CHURCH SCHOOLS
& PUBLIC MONEY

24 95

CHURCH SCHOOLS

& PUBLIC MONEY

THE POLITICS
OF PAROCHIAID

EDD DOERR & ALBERT J. MENENDEZ

PROMETHEUS BOOKS
BUFFALO, NEW YORK

For Herenia and Shirley

Published 1991 by Prometheus Books

Church Schools and Public Money: The Politics of Parochiaid. Copyright © 1991
by Edd Doerr and Albert J. Menendez. All rights reserved. No part of this publication
may be reproduced, stored in a retrieval system, or transmitted in any form or by
any means, electronic, mechanical, photocopying, recording, or otherwise, without prior
written permission of the publisher, except in the case of brief quotations embodied
in critical articles and reviews. Inquiries should be addressed to Prometheus Books,
700 East Amherst Street, Buffalo, New York 14215, 716-837-2475. FAX: 716-835-
6901.

95 94 93 92 91   5 4 3 2 1

Library of Congress Cataloging-in-Publication Data

Doerr, Edd.
    Church schools and public money : the politics of parochiaid / Edd Doerr and
Albert J. Menendez.
        p.   cm.
    Includes bibliographical references and index.
    ISBN 0-87975-708-6 (alk. paper)
    1. Church schools—United States—Finance. 2. Federal aid to private schools—
United States. 3. State aid to private schools—United States. I. Menendez,
Albert J. II. Title.
LC377.D64   1991
379.3'22'0973—dc20   91-22383
                                                                          CIP

Published in cooperation with Americans for Religious Liberty, P.O. Box 6656, Silver
Spring, Maryland 20916. Americans for Religious Liberty (ARL) is a nonprofit public-
interest educational organization, founded in 1981, dedicated to preserving the American
tradition of religious, intellectual, and personal freedom in a pluralistic secular democratic
state. Membership is open to all who share that purpose. ARL publishes a newsletter
and other material, operates a speaker bureau, and has been involved in litigation
in defense of separation of church and state and freedom of conscience. Inquiries
are welcomed.

Printed in the United States of America on acid-free paper.

Acknowledgments

We are deeply indebted to the many men and women (Leo Pfeffer, Florence Flast, Paul Blanshard, Gaston D. Cogdell, Glenn L. Archer, to name but a few) whose dedication to religious freedom, public education, and the American constitutional principle of separation of church and state have merited them the gratitude of their fellow citizens.

We wish also to express our deepest appreciation to Marie Gore for her excellent work in keyboarding this book and for suffering through our numerous revisions. Thanks as well to Jack Mayr for providing us with research material.

Finally, our gratitude to the *Valparaiso University Law Review* for permission to adapt parts of chapters 1 and 7 from Edd Doerr's article "The Enduring Controversy: Parochiaid and the Law," which appeared in vol. 9, no. 3.

The tables appearing in this book were developed from data contained in reports published by Quality Education Data, Denver, Colorado, and from *The Supreme Court and Public Funds for Religious Schools,* by Joseph Bryson and Samuel Houston (1990).

Contents

Introduction

Tensions are building anew in the ancient and never-ending controversies over religious freedom, education, and the relation of government and its taxing power to religious institutions. Presidents Ronald Reagan and George Bush, sectarian special interests, politicians bent on aiding these interests, and a bloc of syndicated pundits, economists, and attorneys have stirred up a new campaign to compel all citizens to contribute involuntarily through taxes to the support of nonpublic schools, the overwhelming majority of which are religious institutions.

Unfortunately, the public is normally not very well informed on the issue. This is not to say that voters, when forced to confront the issue in statewide referendum elections, as they often have been during the past quarter century, have not become aware enough almost invariably to defeat proposals to provide tax aid or support for nonpublic schools. But the public debate generally tends to be dominated by the powerful pressure groups and special interests which either are indifferent to our country's heritage of religious freedom and church-state separation or else wish to change that arrangement.

It is our purpose in this book to provide the information needed for informed public debate on this crucial issue, information not readily available from any other source. We examine the statistics on enrollments in public and nonpublic schools and enrollment trends;

9

the nature of nonpublic schools and how they differ profoundly from our democratic, pluralistic public schools; the state referendum elections on tax aid for nonpublic schools, which have received perplexingly little media coverage; the complex federal and state political battles over "parochiaid"; the court rulings on the subject; and, finally, the arguments made for and against tax support for nonpublic schools.

The parochiaid controversy has raged in the United States and other countries for generations. In the main it represents a clash between those who value religious freedom, pluralism, democratic public education, and an open society, on the one hand, and those who, on the other, would revive sectarian antagonisms, fragment society, entangle religion and government, and replace democratic education with special interest indoctrination.

The outcome of the parochiaid battles of the 1990s will help determine the kind of society and country we will bequeath to coming generations. Whether it will be an open, democratic, forward-looking society or a more closed, more feudalized, backward-looking society will be decided by an informed citizenry.

1

Background to the Dispute

The most enduring, bitter, and important controversy in the history of education and church-state relations concerns public funding for religious and other private schools. "Parochiaid"—any form of direct or indirect public aid for parochial and other nonpublic elementary and secondary schools—became a household word after being coined by Michigan journalists during the struggles in that state in the late 1960s. Innumerable battles have taken place in Congress and state legislatures over proposals to provide tax aid in one form or another for nonpublic schools. Referenda have been held on the subject in recent years in New York, Massachusetts, Michigan, California, Oregon, and the District of Columbia. Rivers of ink and thousands of hours of radio and television time have been devoted to it. Federal and state courts have been blitzed with lawsuits challenging the various parochiaid plans that have gained legislative approval. The United States Supreme Court has handed down a series of rulings on the subject. After a decade or so of relative quiet, following the defeat of a major parochiaid effort in Congress in 1977–78, the controversy has resurfaced with explosive intensity.

In this chapter we shall review some of the landmark court decisions affecting the permitting of prayers in public schools against the background of public education in the United States. With this we shall examine how the framers of the Constitution saw the church-state controversy and how they intended to resolve it. But we may begin with a broad comparison between educational systems in this country and those in Canada and nations abroad, noting some salient differences (and growing similarities).

A COMPARATIVE LOOK AT PUBLIC EDUCATION

In England Adam Smith urged free, compulsory education for the "inferior ranks of the people" as a state function.[1] Thomas Malthus and Thomas Paine also urged the creation of public schools.[2] Public funds began flowing to private Church of England schools in 1833 and to Roman Catholic and Methodist schools after 1847. By 1870, the British government was supplying £500,000 annually to Anglican schools and £200,000 to Roman Catholic, Methodist, and other private schools. It was not until after 1870 that Britain established what Americans call public schools, a development long delayed by conservative and religious opposition. Today English and Welsh public or county schools enroll three-quarters of the eligible students while Anglican, Roman Catholic, and dissenting church schools enroll nearly all the rest. The church schools are generously, though not completely, funded from tax sources. Public schools, incidentally, are required by law to provide "agreed syllabus" religious instruction and daily worship activities.[3]

In Ireland virtually all education is operated by religious bodies and is tax-supported, though in a rather niggardly fashion. Nearly all the schools are Roman Catholic; a few are Protestant and Jewish. In Northern Ireland a modified form of the British system is in operation, with nearly all Catholic children attending tax-supported Catholic schools and the remainder of the children attending public, Protestant-oriented, schools. The almost total religious segregation in Ulster education is regarded by many authorities as an important contributing factor to the bloody unrest there.[4]

Public education was well developed in the Netherlands by 1860, when 79 percent of the students attended public schools. However, Catholic and Reformed Church leaders waged a long campaign to obtain public support for their parochial schools. Their political efforts succeeded, and today a mere quarter of Dutch children attend public schools. Nearly three-quarters are in religiously segregated Catholic and Protestant schools.[5]

In France education was in the hands of the Catholic Church

until the Revolution. Napoleon restored education to the church, but stormy developments in the nineteenth century left education "public, free, compulsory, and secular" by the early 1900s. During World War II Marshall Petain's collaborationist government permitted religious teachers to return to private schools; by the late 1950s the DeGaulle government began public subsidies for Catholic schools.[6]

The states (*Länder*) in what was until 1990 West Germany have developed a variety of ways of organizing and funding education. While the patterns of organization and funding are quite complex, two common features are denominational public schools and considerable state aid for private religious schools. Interestingly, a large and growing number of German Catholic parents express a preference for secular schooling over either parochial schools or confessional public schools.[7] (In addition, the vast majority of German citizens pay a hefty church tax, about 9 percent of their national income tax.)

The Canadian provinces tend to imitate European models of education. Quebec and Newfoundland have only denominational schools, which are publicly supported; Ontario, Alberta, Saskatchewan, and British Columbia have American-sytle public school systems with some publicly supported sectarian schools.[8] Substantial federal and state aid flows to Catholic and other parochial schools in Australia, although there have been divisive political struggles over this aid.[9] A constitutional challenge before the country's highest court failed in 1981, and parochial schools now receive proportionately greater federal funding than public schools.

THE EMERGENT MODEL OF AMERICAN PUBLIC SCHOOLS

The nations that sent the bulk of immigrants to our shores evolved school systems and church-state relations quite different from the model that has developed from diverse beginnings in this country.

Beginning in 1607, an improbable collection of people began settling on the eastern shore of North America. They came from England, Scotland, Ireland, France, Germany, Sweden, the Netherlands, Africa, and elsewhere. Among them were Congregationalists (Puritans and Pilgrims), Anglicans, Roman Catholics, Baptists, Methodists, Lutherans, Presbyterians, Jews, Quakers, Mennonites, Moravians, and Dutch

Reformed. A large number of them came here for greater religious freedom, although most of the colonies they set up practiced varying degrees of intolerance toward dissenters and generally provided tax support for religion.[10]

From humble beginnings these disparate peoples evolved into the most prosperous, technologically advanced, and free nation in the world. Central to this process was the development of nonsectarian public school systems and the generally accepted constitutional principle of separation of church and state.

The separation principle, although articulated in the early seventeenth century by Roger Williams,[11] had to wait for Thomas Jefferson, James Madison, and other Virginians to be put into operation. In the same year that the Declaration of Independence was signed, the Virginia legislature took the first steps to disestablish the Anglican Church and expand religious freedom.[12] Since these steps did not go far enough, Jefferson, Madison, and Baptist and Presbyterian leaders began a drive to completely separate church and state. Their efforts led to the passage in 1786 of Jefferson's Bill for Establishing Religious Freedom. This Act ended legal compulsion to attend church and barred tax support for religious institutions. It also provided that "no man . . . shall be enforced, restrained, molested, or burdened in his body or goods, nor shall otherwise suffer on account of his religious opinions or beliefs, but that all men shall be free to profess, and by argument to maintain, their opinions in matters of religion, and that the same shall in no wise diminish, enlarge, or affect their civil capacities."[13]

By the time the First Amendment to the United States Constitution was adopted in 1791, all the states guaranteed religious liberty to a large extent and only four retained substantial vestiges of religious establishments.[14] Massachusetts finally gave up its establishment of religion in 1833.[15] As Leo Pfeffer has pointed out, the movement toward separation of church and state began with gradual extensions of religious liberty, then saw single establishments give way to multiple establishments, and ended with the cessation of all tax aid for religious institutions.[16] Pfeffer adds:

> It is important to note that in no case did the development end until complete disestablishment was arrived at: no state stopped with according freedom of worship, or indeed with less than complete prohibition of tax support of any and all religions. Moreover, every state

that entered the Union after the Constitution was adopted incorporated both prohibitions in its constitution or basic laws. In no case was there any attempt to establish any denomination or religion; on the contrary, in varying language but with a single spirit, all states expressly forbade such attempts. This deliberate decision was not motivated by indifference to religion: most of the states had been settled by deeply religious pioneers. Nor was it dictated by purely practical considerations; many of the states had a population far·more homogeneous religiously than Canada, Holland, or even England. . . . The decision was in all cases voluntary; and it was made because the unitary principle of separation and freedom was as integral a part of American democracy as republicanism, representative government, and freedom of expression.[17]

Not only did the first thirteen states all follow the example set by Virginia and the First Amendment, but "from 1876 onward all new states added to the Union were required by Congress to include in their basic laws an irrevocable ordinance guaranteeing religious freedom in line with the First Amendment."[18]

While the Constitution drafted in 1787 did not grant the federal government power to deal with religion in any way; and proscribed religious tests for public office, thus implying the principle of separation of church and state, the absence of a specific, explicit religious freedom guarantee still troubled Jefferson and many other citizens. Six states ratified the Constitution but insisted on religious freedom amendments. Rhode Island and North Carolina declined to ratify it until a bill of rights guaranteeing religious liberty was adopted.[19]

Shortly after his election to the House of Representatives in 1789, Madison introduced a compilation of proposals for a bill of rights to be added to the Constitution by amendment. Several versions of a religious liberty provision were debated before the following wording of what is now the First Amendment was adopted: "Congress shall make no law respecting an establishment of religion, or prohibiting the free exercise thereof. . . ."[20]

Jefferson, in a carefully thought-out letter of 1802 to the Danbury Baptist Association, declared that these words built a "wall of separation between church and state."[21] Church-state separationists generally hold that the First Amendment's "no establishment" clause was best and most succinctly interpreted by the Supreme Court in *Everson* v. *Board of Education* in 1947. In *Everson* the Court stated:

The "establishment of religion" clause of the First Amendment means at least this: neither a state nor the federal government can set up a church. Neither can pass laws which aid one religion, aid all religions, or prefer one religion over another. Neither can force nor influence a person to go to or remain away from church against his will or force him to profess a belief or disbelief in any religion. No person can be punished for entertaining or professing religious beliefs or disbeliefs, for church attendance or nonattendance. No tax in any amount, large or small, can be levied to support any religious activities or institutions, whatever they may be called, or whatever form they may adopt to teach or practice religion. Neither a state nor the federal government can, openly or secretly, participate in the affairs of any religious organizations or groups and vice versa. In the words of Jefferson, the clause against establishment of religion by law was intended to erect "a wall of separation between Church and State."[22]

A contrasting point of view was expressed by the National Catholic Welfare Conference in a 1948 statement asserting that the "no establishment" clause was intended only to prevent the setting up of a single established or preferred church.[23] Pfeffer, however, shows that the weight of evidence favors the Court's *Everson* interpretation.[24]

The First Amendment prohibition against laws respecting establishments of religion at first applied only to the federal government, but in 1940 the Supreme Court made it clear that "the Fourteenth Amendment has rendered the legislatures of the states as incompetent as Congress to enact such laws."[25]

THE AMERICAN PUBLIC SCHOOL

While it would be impossible to do justice to the complex history of public education in this country in anything less than a sizable volume, a brief capsule treatment is necessary to put the parochiaid controversy in perspective.

During the colonial period, American education was almost entirely a religious and private affair. In Puritan New England, where church and state were often inextricably intertwined, education was a quasi-religious, quasi-public operation. In the middle colonies, with their greater religious diversity, parochial education was the rule. In the Anglican south, what education there was was mainly private. Pauper schools were developed for the poor who could not afford parochial or private schooling. As religious tolerance and pluralism grew, the church gradually faded from the New England educational scene and the community-controlled public school evolved, setting the basic pattern for the rest of the country. Following the political and economic upheavals of the late eighteenth and early nineteenth centuries, parochial and private education gradually diminished as true public schools appeared, grew, and proliferated.[26]

Early nineteenth-century public schools tended to be somewhat religious in orientation. Horace Mann and other educational leaders struggled successfully to move the schools to a position of nondenominationalism, at least vis-à-vis most Protestant denominations. Protestant Bible reading and prayers that discriminated against the growing number of Catholic and Jewish children were common and were generally upheld by state courts. Catholic children were sometimes punished or expelled from school for refusing to participate in essentially Protestant exercises.[27] As early as 1872 the Ohio Supreme Court held, however, that a school board *could* exclude Bible reading.[28] In 1910 the Illinois Supreme Court, in a case brought by Catholic parents of children in public schools, held that school-mandated or sponsored Bible reading was constitutionally prohibited religious instruction, even when dissenting children could opt out of participation.[29] An increasingly pluralistic population not only exerted pressure on the schools to move ever closer to religious neutrality, but also insured that the courts would eventually have to settle the continuing disputes.

In 1948 the Supreme Court ruled in *McCollum* v. *Board of Education* that voluntary "released time" religious instruction held in public schools violated the First Amendment,[30] although four years later the Court would hold that such instruction, if held off public school premises, was not constitutionally prohibited.[31] In 1962 the Court decided in *Engel* v. *Vitale* that recitation in public schools of a prayer formulated by the New York State Board of Regents violated the First Amendment, holding that "it is no part of the business of goverment to compose official prayers for any groups of American people to recite as part of a religious program carried on by the government."[32] The following year the Court struck down state-mandated Bible reading and recitation of the Lord's Prayer in *Abington School District* v. *Schempp*.[33] Religious censorship of public school curriculum content was dealt a blow in 1968 when the Court struck down an

Arkansas law designed to prevent the exposure of students to the theory of evolution.[34]

The Court, in ruling unconstitutional religious instruction and devotional activities in public schools, was neither exhibiting hostility toward religion nor prohibiting the public schools from dealing with it in ways that do not violate the First Amendment. The Court pointed out in *Schempp,* for example, that the Bible may be used as a reference work or studied for its literary or historic qualities and that the schools may offer teaching *about* religion objectively and neutrally, as distinguished from the teaching *of* religion.

Attempts have been made since *Engel* and *Schempp* to persuade Congress to approve proposed amendments to the Constitution that would permit "voluntary" or "nondenominational" prayer in public schools. Responsible religious leaders have tended to oppose such amendments, and they have failed to win approval in either house of Congress. Those opposing such amendments have generally pointed out that truly voluntary prayer by students has never been prohibited by the courts, that any government-sponsored prayers will inevitably violate the rights of minorities, and that no agreement is possible as to what constitutes a "nondenominational" prayer. Bizarre proposals to limit the jurisdiction of the federal courts over controversies involving "voluntary" prayer in public schools have been introduced in Congress. These bills attempted, under the authority of Article III, Section 2 of the Constitution, to deny aggrieved parents and students access to federal courts to challenge possible First Amendment violations.[35]

Over the years, then, the American people have developed a host of local public school systems about which Justice William J. Brennan could write in his concurring opinion in *Schempp*:

> The public schools are supported entirely, in most communities, by public funds—funds exacted not only from parents, nor alone from those who hold particular religious views, nor indeed from those who subscribe to any creed at all. It is implicit in the history and character of American public education that the public schools serve a uniquely public function: the training of American citizens in an atmosphere free of parochial, divisive, or separatist influence of any sort—an atmosphere in which children may assimilate a heritage common to all American groups and religions. This is a heritage neither theistic nor atheistic, but simply civic and patriotic.[36]

NOTES

1. Ellwood P. Cubberley, *The History of Education* (New York: Houghton Mifflin, 1948), pp. 620–21.

2. Ibid., pp. 621–22.

3. Ibid., pp. 633–50; A. Stafford Clayton, *Religion and Schooling* (Blaisdell Division, Ginn and Co., 1969), pp. 11–93; John P. White, "Catholic Education in England," in *Catholic Education in the Western World*, James Michael Lee, ed. (Notre Dame, Ind.: University of Notre Dame Press, 1967), pp. 209–50.

4. Albert J. Menendez, *The Bitter Harvest* (Washington, D.C.: Robert B. Luce, 1973), pp. 69–119.

5. Clayton, *Religion and Schooling*, pp. 100–80; Albert J. Menendez, "Church and State in the Netherlands," *Church & State* 27 (November 1974):3, 6–8; Josephus J. Gielen and W. J. G. M. Gielen, "Catholic Education in the Netherlands," in Lee, *Catholic Education in the Western World*, pp. 113–54.

6. Didier J. Piveteau, "Catholic Education in France," in Lee, *Catholic Education in the Western World*, pp. 1–60; Cubberley, *The History of Education*, pp. 588–603; Albert J. Menendez, "Church and State in France," *Church & State* 28 (January 1975): 13–17.

7. Franz Pöggeler, "Catholic Education in Germany," in Lee, *Catholic Education in the Western World*, pp. 61–112.

8. Edd Doerr, "Canadian, German Experience Supports U.S. System," *Church & State* 21 (September 1968): 19.

9. Stephen Graves, "Parochiaid Down Under," *Church & State* 21 (December 1970): 19.

10. Leo Pfeffer, *Church, State, and Freedom* (Boston: Beacon Press, 1967), pp. 71–90.

11. Ibid., pp. 84–88.

12. Ibid., pp. 91–109.

13. Ibid., pp. 109–14.

14. Ibid., pp. 115–21.

15. Anson Phelps Stokes and Leo Pfeffer, *Church and State in the United States* (New York: Harper & Row, 1964), pp. 76–78.

16. Pfeffer, *Church, State, and Freedom*, pp. 140–42.

17. Ibid., p. 142.

18. R. Freeman Butts, *The American Tradition in Religion and Education* (Boston: Beacon Press, 1950), pp. 102–104.

19. Pfeffer, *Church, State, and Freedom*, pp. 125–27.

20. Ibid.,pp. 126–27.

21. Ibid., p. 133.

22. 330 U.S. 1 (1947).

23. Pfeffer, *Church, State, and Freedom*, p. 151.

24. Ibid., pp. 149–80.

25. *Cantwell* v. *Connecticut*, 310 U.S. 296 (1940).

26. Cubberley, *The History of Education*, pp. 356–75, 497–98, 519–27, 653–708.

27. Pfeffer, *Church, State, and Freedom*, pp. 436–66.

28. *Board of Education of Cincinnati* v. *Minor*, 23 Ohio State 211 (1872).

29. *People ex rel. Ring* v. *Board of Education*, 245 Illinois 234, 92 N.E. 251 (1910).

30. 333 U.S. 203 (1948).

31. *Zorach* v. *Clausen*, 343 U.S. 306 (1952).

32. 370 U.S. 421 (1962).

33. 374 U.S. 203 (1963).

34. *Epperson* v. *Arkansas*, 393 U.S. 97 (1968).

35. "Dangerous Bills," *Church & State* 28 (April 1975): 5, 15.

36. 374 U.S. 203 (1963).

2

The Nature of Church Schools

Understanding the controversy over public or tax aid for nonpublic schooling requires some acquaintance with the nature of nonpublic education. Let us begin by adducing some prominent examples.

Over 90 percent of the students in nonpublic schools attend religious schools. While the term "parochial" does not accurately describe all religious schools, it is the most commonly used and convenient designation. These schools differ radically from the pluralistic, religiously neutral public schools which enroll nine out of ten American children. Otto Kraushaar, who is sympathetic to parochial and private schools and favors tax aid for them, observes that "Catholic, Protestant, and Jewish schools continue to conceive their religious mission as central, and as transcending even their growing commitment to academic learning."[1]

CATHOLIC EDUCATION

The Reverend John L. McKenzie, chairman of the theology department and professor of theology at the University of Notre Dame, describes the Catholic school distinction in this way:

The Roman Catholic schools have always placed religious education as the primary purpose of the schools with no attempt to mask this under some other purpose. . . . The principle on which church educa-

21

tion is conducted goes far beyond formal religious instruction. Children also learn the way of worship; they are taught respect and reverence for prelates, clergy, and religious. They are daily reminded of their identity as Catholics. They grow up in an atmosphere of Roman Catholic traditions and attitudes which are communicated not so much by instruction as by prolonged close association under the direction of professional religious persons.[2]

The Reverend Neil G. McCluskey, dean of teacher education at Lehman College of the City University of New York, points out that religion pervades the parochial school curriculum, "particularly in literature, history, and the social studies." He adds that "the function of the Catholic school is not merely to teach the formulas of the Catholic religion but . . . 'to impart in a thousand ways, which defy formularization, the Catholic attitude toward life as a whole.' "[3]

That the Catholic school should be a pervasively religious institution was stressed by Pope Pius XI in his 1929 encyclical on the *Christian Education of Youth*:

The mere fact that a school gives some religious instruction (often extremely stinted) does not bring it into accord with the rights of the Church and the Christian family or make it a fit place for Catholic education. To be this it is necessary that all the teaching and the whole organization of the school, and its teachers, syllabus, and textbooks in every branch, be regulated by the Christian Spirit, under the direction and maternal supervision of the Church; so that Religion may be in very truth the foundation and crown of the youth's entire training; and this in every grade of school, not only the elementary, but the intermediate and the higher institutions of learning as well. "For it is necessary," if we may use the words of Leo XIII (Enc. *Militantis Ecclesiae*, 1897) "not only at certain hours to teach Catholic religion to children but that all other subjects must also be made fragrant with the odor of piety. If this be not done, if this holy habit should not pervade and permeate the souls of both teachers and pupils, little benefit will accrue from any teaching but generally very great harm.[4]

PROTESTANT EDUCATION

Protestant schools emphasize a similar inculcation of religious values. Professor Harry C. Coiner of Concordia Theological Seminary describes Missouri Synod Lutheran schools as follows:

> The church-related school, which does not face the problem of religious pluralism and is free to teach Biblical doctrines, can do much more specific work in Christian education.
>
> The [Lutheran] school enables the child to experience a totally Christ-centered program, a program which focuses the application of God's word on him and on all areas of his life.
>
> The relationship of science, social studies, language, arithmetic, and other subjects to Biblical truth may be taught without limitation.
>
> Daily social contact between teachers and pupils of the same Christian faith reinforces learning by attitude and example. The absence of any formal educational influence that is strange, foreign, or antagonistic in any way to the positive Christian educational process permits the building of one stone on another without destructive influence.[5]

Other denominational schools are similarly religious in theory and practice.

Parents send children to parochial schools primarily for religious reasons. Kraushaar concludes that these parents attach little importance to educational innovations, "social advantages," or "better educational buildings and equipment," but do place a great deal of importance on the fact that "the typical nonpublic school is founded to serve and is supported by a cohesive ideological community based on religious, social, academic, or racial interests, rather than to serve a neighborhood or district of the general community as the public school does."[6]

Catholic schools, by far the largest and most important sector of nonpublic education, grew until they reached a peak enrollment of about 5.6 million in 1965 and then, alone among nonpublic school systems, began a pronounced decline which reduced enrollment to about 2.6 million in 1989-90. A Boston College study done for former President Richard Nixon's Commission on School Finance explained that the decline of anti-Catholic prejudice and social exclusion largely accounts for the shift from parochial to public schools.[7]

In fact, an estimated 70 to 75 percent of Catholic children now attend public schools.

What is true for Catholic schools is true also for Protestant schools. Indeed, the liberalization of curriculum and the more ecumenical approach to religion in Catholic schools make many of the Protestant schools, by contrast, distinctive in their adherence to traditional dogmatic certitudes.

In their book *The Amish School*, Sara E. Fisher and Rachel K. Stahl observe that "religion is taught all day long in the lessons and on the playground. The goal of the Amish schools is to prepare children for usefulness by preparing them for eternity. Each morning, devotions are held. The Bible is read and the Lord's Prayer is repeated in unison."[8]

Furthermore, Amish schools reflect and are pervaded by Amish values. "An Amish child is not taught to have selfish needs of privacy, space, recognition and admiration, ambition and rewards that a child in large society absorbs as its birthright."[9] They are not encouraged to study beyond the eighth grade. "An Amish child has an enormous sense of security in community. Leaving that security for the fleeting pleasure of higher education is not only risky but fearsome for most."[10]

Textbooks are carefully selected. Since 1948 the Old Order Book Society in Lancaster County, Pennsylvania, reprints textbooks long since discarded by public schools but considered "wholesome" by the Amish.[11] Fisher and Stahl maintain that "much of the secular school curricula taught evolution, technology, sex education, and other values contrary to Amish beliefs."[12]

The U.S. Supreme Court, it is true, sustained the values and program of Amish education in the 1972 *Wisconsin* v. *Yoder* decision. It is also true that Amish schools do not want public financing of their educational enterprise. However, the kind of education imparted to Amish children is typical of parochial schools founded by German-American Protestant sectarians, many of whom do seek parochiaid.

CHURCH-RUN PRIVATE SCHOOLS AND PUBLIC MORALITY

We have reviewed some examples of how doctrinalism pervades all facets of instruction in sectarian schools. Let us now look at the area of discipline and questions relating to religious belief and practice in church-run private education. We can offer several examples.

Michael Kremm, chairman for over five years of the religion department at Gabriel Richard High School, a Catholic academy in Ann Arbor, Michigan, was forced to resign in 1982 because he and his wife had their daughter baptized in a United Methodist church. School officials explained the teacher might have survived if he had not "gone public" and admitted that his daughter was not being raised in the Catholic Church. School policy requires teachers to "support and exemplify in conduct and instruction both Catholic doctrine and morality."[13]

Vickie McIntyre, a sixth grader at Our Lady of Lourdes School in Decatur, Illinois, was expelled from school in 1982 because her mother did not attend Sunday Mass regularly. The girl's mother explained that she worked two jobs and could not attend. School policy requires that Catholic parents attend church regularly as a condition of the children's enrollment. Bishop Joseph McNicholas of the Springfield diocese refused the parents' requests to intervene, saying, "I have no intention of interfering with Father Sullivan's operation of Our Lady of Lourdes parish and school."[14]

Susan Long Little, a divorced Protestant teacher who had taught successfully for nine years at St. Mary Magdalene School in Pittsburgh, was fired after she married her second husband, a nonpracticing Catholic, in a civil ceremony. Church officials said she was not rehired for the 1987–88 school year because she failed to undergo required ecclesiastical procedures that would have allowed her to remarry validly in the eyes of the church. Apparently, Pittsburgh Bishop Donald P. Wuerl had engineered her ouster.

Mrs. Little sued for violation of her civil rights. But a federal appeals court ruled that Title VII of the Federal Civil Rights Act of 1964 does not apply when a parochial school decides to "discharge a Catholic or a non-Catholic teacher who has publicly engaged in conduct regarded by the school as inconsistent with its religious principles."[15]

Linda Hoskinson, a teacher at the fundamentalist Dayton Christian School in Ohio, was dismissed in 1979 after school authorities learned that she was pregnant, although she was already married. These fundamentalists believe that the Bible requires mothers of school-age children to refrain from working outside the home. When she protested and consulted an attorney, the school fired her for violating the "biblical chain of command." Thereafter, she fought her dismissal before the Ohio Civil Rights Commission and eventually the U.S. Supreme Court, which held in 1986 that she could challenge her firing before the state's civil rights commission. (The school had tried to invoke the principle of church-state separation but the Supreme Court disagreed.) Hoskinson complained that while the school tried to avoid state regulation in its hiring practices, it accepted state aid. In 1987 she chose to withdraw her complaint.[16]

In 1987 a North Carolina court ordered the Goldsboro Christian School to reinstate a seventeen-year-old senior who had been expelled two months before graduation because she had modeled swimsuits in a local department store. The school's "ruling pastor" (headmaster) said the student had given the school a bad image. The same school was involved in a 1983 U.S. Supreme Court ruling that held that religious schools practicing racial discrimination could be denied tax exemption. At that time Goldsboro Christian School refused to admit black students.[17]

Cases such as these indicate that church-run schools can enforce on faculty, parents, and students sectarian standards that are forbidden in public schools, since the latter are accountable to the community and not to the strictures of any religious group.

In his coverage of the 1983 annual convention of the National Catholic Educational Association, Religious News Service reporter William Bole summed up his review of the activities:

> Catholic educators admit they'd like it both ways. On one hand, with the extraordinary growth in the number of minorities and non-Catholics in church-run schools, they are saying that parochial schools really are nonsectarian. The schools, they say, make broad social contributions to American society, and thus deserve government aid.
>
> Yet, church leaders have also set out at the same time to make parochial schools more "Catholic." The move comes in response not only to the wishes of Catholic parents but to the startling fact that now only one-fourth of their teachers are priests or nuns. And the effort, church leaders say, involves viewing non-Catholic pupils as potential converts.[18]

A number of church educators have called for increased "evangelization" of the 10 percent of Catholic school students who are not

Catholic. Bishop John S. Cummins of Oakland, California, encouraged this trend and noted an increase in conversions in his diocesan school system, which is 44 percent non-Catholic. Reverend Alvin Illig, who directs a Catholic evangelism office, has called parochial schools "one of the great tools of evangelization."[19]

The most important affirmation of this position has come from Pope John Paul II in a 1984 address. The pope told Catholic educators, "The school is an essential instrument for the spreading of faith, for the expansion of Christianity and the reign of God. For this reason the school is for this Church a reason for life."[20]

All church-related schools cite religious belief and practice as major factors in the decision to maintain separate educational institutions. A Seventh-Day Adventist educator has observed, "Seventh-Day Adventist education is basically a church-supported program. Aside from the tuition and fees paid by students and their parents, the bulk of the financial support comes from the local churches and supporting organizations."[21] He continues:

> The public schools cannot provide teachers who can teach their disciplines and at the same time relate them to religion and religious life. . . . Adventists believe that their young people must not only be trained and educated to live and to make a contribution in this world, but they must also be readied for the great Advent, and of course there are other approaches that could not be taken in a public system but which would be quite common in a Christian school.
>
> Every school system must have specific goals and objectives. Those of the Seventh-Day Adventist schools include the development of the spiritual or religious which are paramount and which must permeate the pupils' total program. They must demonstrate a good understanding of the Scriptures and be knowledgeable in the doctrines of the church.[22]

Similar views are expressed by two Lutheran spokespersons. Allan H. Jahnsmann, a member of the Board of Parish Education of the Lutheran Church Missouri Synod (LCMS), has spelled out the theological foundations of Lutheran schools in his monograph, "What's Lutheran in Education?" He points out that the Lutheran doctrine of the Scriptures "demands . . . that the Bible be dominant not only as basic subject matter, but also as a dynamic frame of reference and an orienting force which Christianizes every other subject in a curriculum."[23]

Dr. Paul Lange of the LCMS Board of Christian Education stated in 1950 that "In the [Lutheran] Christian view, there can be no artificial divorce between sacred and secular learning . . . Christian doctrine will, therefore, permeate the entire program."[24]

Roman Catholic scholars at the National Opinion Research Center exhaustively surveyed their church's parochial school system in the mid-1970s. Their conclusions, presented in *Catholic Schools in a Declining Church* by Andrew M. Greeley, William C. McCready, and Kathleen McCourt, are important to the debate over parochiaid.

The percentage of school-age children from Catholic families attending parochial schools declined from 44 percent in 1964 to 29 percent in 1974, even though a large majority of Catholics interviewed (80 percent) indicated that they would give $1.8 billion more each year to save the parochial school system from its present crisis. In 1974, 46 percent of Catholic children living in cities were attending parochial schools, compared to 27 percent in small town and rural areas, and 20 percent in suburbs. Greeley, McCready, and McCourt maintain that disillusionment with the 1968 papal encyclical on birth control, the church's position on divorce and remarriage, and the lack of credible hierarchical leadership have produced a massive decline in church attendance, doctrinal orthodoxy, institutional loyalty, and, significantly, voluntary financial contribution to the church. "It is not that the people are unable to give money to the church; they are able to and they do not want to. If people had given to the church in 1974 at the same rate they did in 1963, they would have contributed over $5.6 billion instead of the $3.8 billion actually given. It is certainly a logical possibility that this could have happened, since the income and total population of the Catholic community have gone up. There was no extra sacrifice needed to keep the level of giving at the same rate," they concluded.[25]

Despite this, the main reason cited for the declining use of parochial schools, according to this study, is their unavailability in the fast-growing suburban areas where so many Catholics now live. More of those surveyed gave this as the reason for nonuse of parochial schools rather than increasing costs or preference for public education. While the study concurs with the Notre Dame and Boston College studies done for former President Nixon's Commission on School Finance in that the decline of parochial enrollment is not due primarily to economic factors, the authors disagree with the finding of the

1971 Boston College study, *Issues of Aid to Nonpublic Schools*, that the decline is due chiefly to changing parental preferences: "The Americanization process has deflated the necessity of the Catholic school system as the primary agency for religious education, particularly in the minds of the younger, better-educated members of the Church."[26]

Those who choose parochial schools do so for a variety of reasons, primarily for religious instruction or presumed academic excellence. Parochial school graduates do not differ substantially from Catholic graduates of public schools, except in church attendance in adulthood and somewhat greater religious knowledge. Among young men attendance at parochial schools has diminished the tendency to disaffiliate from the church in adulthood. "The schools are more critical to the church now than they were a decade ago for two reasons: they prevent losses where losses are most likely to be the worst, among men and among the young."[27]

The above data are convincing evidence that parochial school problems are internal church problems which must be resolved within the Catholic community. Taxpayers of other faiths or, for that matter, of the Catholic faith, should not be called upon to solve intra-church problems.

At about the same time that the Greeley survey appeared, Milo Brekke's study, *How Different Are People Who Attended Lutheran Schools?* provided a similar analysis of Missouri Synod Lutheran schools and their relationship to the Lutheran community. He found that 38 percent of church members had attended parochial schools for some or all of their education.

Lutheran schooling made a difference in certain aspects of behavior, particularly in the religious realm. Students who attended Lutheran schools have a much deeper commitment to the church and a much greater knowledge of the Bible. As adults, they pray and attend church more frequently and are more concerned with sharing their faith with others. (Brekke compared parochial school graduates with public school graduates within the Lutheran community.)

On the other hand, he concluded, parochial school attendance "does not decrease desire to remain socially distant from many disadvantaged and less fortunate groups and individuals, nor does it reduce prejudice." Furthermore, parochial school graduates do not show evidence of "increased social concern" and are "no more involved in community leadership or personal service to other individuals than are other church members."[28]

A 1966 study of Lutheran schools[29] found that parochial education was only marginally influential. Parochial and public school students of Lutheran faith were remarkably similar in church attendance, belief, willingness to share their faith, stewardship, and social attitudes. Such studies leave little doubt that Lutheran schools are primarily religious institutions which transmit and reinforce distinctively denominational values and lifestyles.

Still, Lutheran schools retained their appeal, and began to gain students in the late 1970s and early 1980s. Interestingly, the percentage of non-Lutherans increased sharply, from 26 percent in 1972 to 40.6 percent in 1982.[30] Lutheran pastor Jon Diefenthaler has suggested that Lutheran schools may have to change to accommodate these new pupils of other traditions. He observes: "Does a classroom consisting of many non-Lutheran pupils require adjustments in a curriculum traditionally designed to inculcate sound Lutheran doctrine? How do Lutheran teachers relate to children and families who do not share their allegiance to certain religious beliefs? The sacramental view of Holy Baptism that Lutherans assert would seem to be a very sensitive matter for those Protestants who insist upon a believer's approach to the subject."[31] But in the final analysis, the religious dimension of Lutheran schools is what makes them appealing, Diefenthaler concludes. "The Christian aspects of the training offered in Lutheran schools no doubt appeal to certain evangelical Protestants, especially those who believe that America is on the brink of moral bankruptcy."[32]

Church-related schools advertise themselves to prospective patrons in ways that clearly emphasize religious values. The Christian Reformed School Association, for example, placed an advertisement in 1984 in the *Grand Rapids Press* proclaiming that "Christian schools believe that God made everything. That's why they see him in math, history, science, and English and in all the other subjects they teach."

The Capitol Christian Academy in Upper Marlboro, Maryland, tells its potential students and their parents, in an advertisement, that it offers "dedicated Christian instructors and strong discipline" to "train young people to walk with God."

In his ethnographic study of a Midwestern fundamentalist Christian school, Alan Peshkin argued that such schools are all-encompassing, totalistic institutions which seek to mold individuals in accordance with a unitary approach to life. The school he studied, Bethany Baptist Academy, was "a total institution, the natural organizational outcome of a school based on absolute truth."[33]

Peshkin explained that the school's published purposes, and those of the American Association of Christian Schools, are decidedly sectarian. They are: to bring children to salvation; to inform children about the Word of God; to keep children immersed in God; to keep children separate from the world; to encourage children to proselytize the unsaved; to lead children into service as preachers, teachers, and evangelists; and to have children become fully committed Christians, living their lives first and foremost for the glory of God.[34]

Peshkin also found that the academy's teachers and principal conceive their roles as more missionary than academic. He found that secular and religious values interacted and reinforced each other. He was also disturbed that the school's narrow approach to religion would lead many of its graduates to live their entire lives in religious ghettoes and to regard those of other faiths as threats to their existence rather than as neighbors and friends.

Additional studies corroborate Peshkin's analysis. Paul A. Klenel, executive director of the Association of Christian Schools International, a federation of American evangelical schools, asserted uncompromisingly in 1977 that "Christian schools are Christian institutions, where Jesus Christ and the Bible are central in the school curriculum and in the lives of teachers and administrators."[35]

Mississippi State University Professor James C. Carper, in his study of Christian separate schools, explained this burgeoning phenomenon. "Since the mid-1960s, evangelical Protestants and their churches have been establishing Christian day schools at a phenomenal rate. Several proponents of these institutions have claimed, perhaps with some exaggeration, that Christian schools are being established at the rate of nearly two per day. Not only do these schools currently constitute the most rapidly expanding segment of formal education in the United States, but they also represent the first widespread secession from the public school pattern since the establishment of Catholic schools in the nineteenth century."[36] Carper adds: "Studies of the reasons parents send their children to such schools point consistently to their desire for a Christ-centered or Bible-centered academic program."[37]

Carper states that while these schools vary widely in academic quality, social status, equipment, and course offerings, they share a central viewpoint. He says: "Although these institutions are diverse in many respects, they all profess the centrality of Jesus Christ and the Bible in their educational endeavors. Regardless of the subject matter, a conservative Christian perspective is usually employed."[38]

Another type of conservative Protestant school educates about 75,000 students of largely Dutch ancestry in the American Midwest, particularly in Iowa and Michigan. These are the Calvinist-oriented National Union of Christian Schools International, based in Grand Rapids, Michigan. A study of these schools concluded that their unifying feature was "a grounding in biblical/theological principles as seen in Calvinist perspective."[39] Furthermore, "the leaders and spokesmen have over the years forged a web of interrelated doctrines which provide the religious foundations of the movement."[40]

Two values shape these schools, say Opperval and De Boer. "The proper relation between education and religion is not that of neutrality toward all, nor simple indoctrination in one, but the integration of a religious worldview into all curriculum content. The aim of such education is neither evangelization for church membership nor neutral, value-free information-giving, but preparing the learner for living a Christian lifestyle in contemporary society."[41] Calvinist schools also have as a goal "helping young Christians to exercise cultural dominion rather than seeking cultural isolation."[42] Calvinist school textbooks reflect these values and concerns. Opperval and De Boer reveal that religious interpretations permeate all courses, from civics to science to biology, health education, and literature.

The permeation of secular studies by religious doctrinalism can likewise be noted in Seventh-Day Adventist schools. Professor George R. Knight of Andrews University explains how this works in his church's school system. "Adventism has developed a curricular stance that is unashamedly based on biblical revelation and looks at science from the standpoint of creationism. Adventists hold that all truth is essentially religious, and some contemporary educators have given great impetus and publicity to the techniques of integrating all subject matter within the context and worldview of the Bible. The General Conference Department of Education has been active in developing textbooks in such areas as science, reading, social studies, and religion in an attempt to better present the Christian perspective in every classroom subject."[43]

Knight reveals another unusual distinction of Adventist education when he states that Adventist schools "have opted, on the basis of their beliefs, to avoid highly competitive activities. Cooperation rather than competition, they hold, is more in line with the teachings of Jesus. As a result, they have avoided interschool athletic competition."[44]

We have by no means painted a complete portrait of church-connected schools. There are still others. Quaker and Episcopal schools are considered by most authorities to be the least sectarian and the most academically rigorous of church schools. They are less likely to require religious courses or mandatory worship. But, historically, they, too, were established for religious reasons. A study of Quaker schools in Baltimore, for example, found that their purpose was to "provide a guarded education in which students would be exposed to the principles of the Society of Friends."[45] Lawrence A. Cremin says that Quaker education "meant, first, an indoctrination in the history and beliefs of the Society of Friends and, second, a protection from the corrupting influence of the world."[46]

ORTHODOX JEWISH EDUCATION

Orthodox Jewish schools have a clear religious identity and purpose. Eduardo Rauch says that Jewish schools adhere to the following eight educational objectives: to provide knowledge of the classical Jewish texts and the traditions embodied therein; to foster a life-long commitment to the study of Torah; to develop some form of personal observance; to develop a facility in the Hebrew language and a familiarity with its literature; to nurture an identification with the Jewish people through a knowledge of its past, and to encourage a concern for its survival and welfare the world over; to stimulate a recognition of the unique place of Israel in the Jewish imagination, both past and present, and to foster the acceptance of some sort of personal obligation to participate in its development; to encourage participation in American society, based on a conscious awareness of the relationship between Jewish tradition and democracy; to inculcate faith in God and trust in his beneficence.[47]

Rauch also points out that "most [Jewish] schools include subjects such as prayer, the first five books of the Bible, learned comments to these five books by the medieval scholar Rashi, prophets,

Hebrew language, arts, laws and customs, history, sections of the Talmud, ethics and Israel."[48] Finally, he notes, "One of the basic features of the day school program is pupil participation in religious activities. . . . Experiences around the religious holidays are regularly planned."[49]

Ari L. Goldman, the religion correspondent of the *New York Times*, describes his education at an Orthodox yeshiva in New York City: "At the right-wing Orthodox high school I attended, there was no acknowledgment that anyone but us, sitting there poring over the Talmud, had any religious validity. Christianity was unmentionable. . . . We were also taught to shun those in the more liberal Reformed and Conservative branches of Judaism. Just as one was not permitted to enter a church (even if only to escape the rain), one could not walk into a Reform or Conservative Temple."[50]

Goldman says that school authorities saw religious knowledge as far more important than secular culture. "Likewise, so-called secular knowledge—math, science, literature—was given second-class status. 'Real' knowledge was knowledge of the Torah; the rest was only a concession to a world into which we would have to go out someday and make a living. College was frowned upon, although the right-wing rabbis looked the other way if you studied Torah during the day and went to college at night."[51]

SECTARIAN SCHOOL TEXTBOOKS

It is hardly surprising that the textbooks used in church schools reflect the values, commitments, and priorities of the sponsoring religious body. George R. LaNoue studied more than one hundred parochial school textbooks and reported his findings.[52] He reached the following conclusions:

1. Religious symbols and subjects are commonly used in mathematics and language arts texts.

2. Specific sectarian doctrines are presented where controversial matter appears in science, geography, and language texts.

3. All subjects are presented with a general Christian theistic approach.

4. Texts in some subjects request that pupils concern themselves with specific church goals, such as working and praying that non-Western cultures will adopt Christianity or playing one's part in spreading the gospel message.

5. Appeals are made to church authority to prove points in many subject areas.

6. Selective emphasis is placed on denominational institutions and contributions to culture and on facts favorable to the particular church, while contributions to culture by other churches and facts unfavorable to the particular church are omitted.

7. Texts in a number of subjects defend denominational social ideas and regulations.

A decade later a priest-scholar, Reverend John T. Pawlikowski, presented a book-length study of Catholic school textbooks conducted by the sociology department of St. Louis University. Pawlikowski concluded that some positive changes had been made, particularly in social studies texts, in the treatment of Protestants and Jews in parochial school materials. Still, a residue of hostility was notable in the religion textbooks. Pawlikowski found patronizing attitudes toward Protestantism and a negative portrayal of Judaism. He argued forcefully that Catholic schools "must eliminate from our instructional materials any residue of the old attitudes. . . ."[53]

The bias in many textbooks designed for fundamentalist Protestant schools is far more pronounced. Even in this era of pluralism in American life, when our nation faces new challenges in assimilating disparate cultures, these texts emphasize a triumphalistic, "America-can-do-no-wrong" view of our national history that excludes all but white Anglo-Saxon Protestants from recognition and appreciation.

Here are some examples. *A Child's Story of America*, published in 1989 by Christian Liberty Press for the Christian Liberty Academy Satellite School System, is suffused with religious and cultural biases. The authors, Michael J. McHugh and Charles Morris, have constructed a history of America for elementary school students which completely ignores Catholics, Jews, immigrants from any nation other than Northern Europe, and even Native Americans, who are disparagingly referred to as Indians throughout the text.

Here is how Native Americans are presented. "These Indians

lived in a very wild fashion. They spent much of their time in hunting, fishing, and fighting. . . . People say that they were badly treated by the European settlers, but they treated one another worse than the settlers ever did."[54]

We provide another reference in the same vein. "The Dutch in New York also had their troubles with the Indians. They paid for all the lands they took, but one of their governors was foolish enough to start a war that went on for two years. Worse trouble started in North Carolina, where there was a powerful tribe called the Tuscaroras. These warriors attacked the settlers and murdered numbers of them. But in the end they were driven out of that part of the country."[55]

The Spanish settlers are treated with contempt. It is mentioned that "some French Protestants tried to settle Florida, but they had been cruelly murdered by the Spaniards."[56] While this is true, it is not mentioned that French and English settlers also attacked the Spanish. As to the fate of Puerto Rico and Cuba in the Spanish-American War, the readers are told that the "Spaniards killed off and robbed the people and have lived on them ever since."[57] However, "with the assistance of the United States government the islands were taken from Spain many years ago."[58] Interestingly, when Spanish, Portuguese, and Italian explorers are mentioned favorably —as in the case of Christopher Columbus—never is it noted that they were Catholics or that clergy accompanied the explorations.

On the other hand, the authors tell the readers, "The Puritans worked hard for the glory of their Lord and Savior Jesus Christ."[59] No mention is made of Puritan persecution of other Christians. Puritan New England is glorified. "In New England, Sunday was kept in a very strict fashion, for the people were very fond of God. It was thought wicked to play or work on the Sabbath. Almost everybody liked to go to church. All who did not go were disciplined. What marvelous sermons they preached in those cold old churches, preaching away sometimes for three or four hours at a time! The boys and girls listened to them, as well as the men and women. It is only natural for Christian people to want to spend as much time as possible in fellowship with God. People today could learn something from these dedicated Christians. They loved God and His law."[60]

The French settlers are treated with disdain. "They were ignorant, simple-minded countrymen, who looked upon France as their country, and were not willing to be British citizens. . . . That is the way with the French. It is the same today in Canada. The descendants of the former French still speak their old language and love their old country. Now they fight the British with their votes as they once did with their swords."[61] In a later section about the Acadians who were expelled from British North America, never is it made clear that they were Catholics forced to leave their homeland largely for religious reasons.

The section on early Maryland is a slight improvement, since Lord Baltimore and the early Catholic settlers are given some credit for allowing a degree of religious freedom to other Christians in their colony. But even this slightly favorable treatment is marred by an oddly inaccurate statement: "All the poor people who came with Lord Baltimore were Protestants. Only the rich ones were Catholics."[62]

America's war with Mexico in the 1840s is seen as wholly just. "Mexico did not feel like giving up Texas so easily, and her rulers said that the United States had no right to take it."[63] But a valiant American army overwhelmed the enemy, and, the text tells us, "When peace was made, the United States claimed the provinces of New Mexico and California, which had been captured by our soldiers. Mexico was paid a large sum of money for these lands. No one then dreamed how rich the provinces were in silver and gold. The provinces of New Mexico and California were later made an official part of the United States."[64]

Every American military venture is treated with awe and wonder. About the Vietnam War we are told, "In 1963, the United States sent soldiers to a small country in Southeast Asia by the name of South Vietnam. The freedom-loving people of South Vietnam were being attacked by Communist soldiers who lived a few miles away in the country of North Vietnam. Millions of dollars were spent each year in an effort to help the people of South Vietnam keep their freedom. Many brave American soldiers died in this sad conflict. The Communist forces were so strong in that part of the world that the United States finally decided to stop fighting in Vietnam during 1973. Several months later the evil force of communism spread into South Vietnam.

"Our nation's fortieth president, Ronald Reagan, was right when he called communism an 'evil system'."[65]

The book ends on a monitory note. The authors warn bluntly;

Indeed, of all the threats that America is facing today, the greatest threat is ungodliness and lawlessness. The basic need of a free society is for its people to be self-governed under God's law. True liberty is not the freedom to live as we please, but the power to live as we know God requires. A corrupt and rebellious people cannot and will not remain free, for the simple reason that such people require a powerful government to pass laws so they can be protected from one another! People will ultimately be ruled voluntarily by God's law (i.e., the Ten Commandments), or they will be ruled forcibly by tyrants."[66]

Another textbook, *New World History and Geography in Christian Perspective*, by Laurel Elizabeth Hicks,[67] designed for secondary school students, reveals the distinctive worldview propagated by many fundamentalist Christians. This book is one of a series of widely popular texts written and distributed by Pensacola Christian College in Florida. A careful reading of this text reveals a pervasive bias that colors the interpretation of historic events in American history and the perception of other nations in the hemisphere. Virtually all political, economic, educational, and social trends or events are seen through a particular religious framework.

First of all, there is a strong religious bias in the interpretation of history. About seventeenth-century England the author says:

By the time that England was ready to send colonists to America, an important change had taken place in England. England had become a Protestant country, and all the important people in England were free to read the Bible for themselves. Queen Elizabeth I passed a law calling for a Bible to be placed in every church. People thronged to the churches to read the Bible, for most people did not yet own a Bible themselves. Those who could not read listened carefully as a man with a strong voice read the Word of God. Bible reading had an important effect on the kind of people who came to America from England and the kind of government they would set up.[68]

Six full pages are devoted to extolling the virtues of the Pilgrims.

The Pilgrims *were* able to govern themselves, because they loved religious freedom and strove for the glory of God. Their love for God and freedom came from their understanding of the Bible and from their English heritage.

There was a lack of freedom in England at this time, even though the English were a freedom-loving people. James I was still the King of England. He said that he was head of the church as well as the head of the government. Because the king forced everyone to attend his church, the Church of England, the people of England were not free to worship as they thought they should."[69]

And further: "These brave people, the Pilgrims, who had such a deep faith in God, were the true heroes of our country's beginnings. We remember them for their courage, for their love of religious freedom, for their establishment of self-government, and for their faith in God and thankfulness to Him."[70]

It is Hicks's opinion that only English Protestants can really govern themselves. "It takes a certain kind of people to be able to make self-government work. It takes the kind of people who are able to control themselves. This is the kind of people that God wants us to be. This is the kind of people the Pilgrims were."[71]

Roger Williams is treated favorably, even though he was a dissenter from the religious Establishment. George Washington is quoted (possibly apocryphally) as praising "the little Baptist state of Rhode Island."[72] Little is said about the religious beliefs of the Dutch, Swedes, Scotch-Irish, or English Cavaliers. There is a mildly favorable treatment of Quaker and Catholic settlers, though the persecution heaped on these two groups is downplayed. The author states, "The founding of Maryland is important because it showed that in America Catholics would be able to worship freely."[73] She does not mention, however, that Catholics soon lost their freedom in Maryland and were ruthlessly persecuted after 1692.

The book shows a clear preference for Puritan New England. "In most homes the Bible was read aloud every night. The Bible could be found in almost every home. Other books, such as *Pilgrim's Progress* and John Foxe's *Book of Martyrs*, were also widely read. But the Bible was the most important book in the lives of most colonists."[74] Much less favorable treatment is given to the Middle Colonies and the Anglican South.

The settlers who built their homes in the Middle Colonies represented many different religions, and the Middle Colonies quickly became known as a land of religious freedom. Many Quakers came to the Middle Colonies to escape the persecution they had faced in England. Other groups who came there included Mennonites, Presbyterians,

Baptists, Anglicans, and Dutch Reformed. In the Middle Colonies, these groups were free to worship God in the way they thought was right.

There were fewer churches in the Southern Colonies than in the other colonies. The Southern colonists planted large farms that separated Southern families from each other. They would have to travel miles each Sunday just to meet. Rather than churches, traveling preachers brought religion to the Southern colonists. Sometimes an Anglican (Church of England) priest would travel around to the farms and perform an Anglican service for the many Southerners who belonged to the Church of England. Later, men called circuit-riding preachers traveled on horseback throughout the South preaching the Bible, and great revivals broke out.

Going to church was the most important part of the week in colonial America. Absolutely no work was done on Sunday; the Sabbath, as it was called, was a special time that all the people honored. Different churches worshiped in different ways, but the services usually included singing, Bible reading, and a long sermon. Most of the services lasted over two hours—some longer than three.[75]

In a later passage, the author clearly shows her nostalgia for an evangelically dominated earlier America. The following passages reveal both bias and inaccuracy.

The public schools were outstanding, and parents could send their children there with confidence, knowing that the values they taught at home would also be taught at school. Many of the public school teachers were Christians, and all of them honored the Bible. Bible reading and prayer were part of the daily routine in each schoolhouse. . . . The Bible was the nation's most honored book. About 100,000 churches dotted the land, and nearly half the people were church members. The majority of the churches were true to the Bible. . . . William McKinley, the President of the United States, was a devout Christian who attended the Methodist church regularly. He took a courageous stand against liquor, swearing, and the telling of dirty stories, and he was known for his personal purity.[76]

Relatively obscure and secondary events in American history are given prominence. More than four pages are devoted to "The Great Awakening," three pages to the "Second Great Awakening," and two pages to late nineteenth-century revivals. These events are considered to be of earth-shaking importance.

One of the most important events in colonial America was the Great Awakening. The leaders of the Great Awakening have been called the spiritual Founding Fathers of America, and their teaching did much to shape the spiritual heritage of America. . . . Many great leaders of England have said that John Wesley did more than perhaps anyone else to make England a strong, free country during a difficult time in her history. The Methodists sent many ministers to America as well, and they played a great part in preaching the Word of God throughout our land.[77]

Baptists and Methodists are the most favorably treated denominations. They always taught the truth while other churches failed to do so. "Many Presbyterian, Congregational, and Dutch Reformed churches were brought back to preaching the gospel," Hicks says.[78] During the Second Great Awakening, "Many people were converted under the preaching of Baptist, Methodist, and Presbyterian evangelists in Indiana, Ohio, Kentucky, and Tennessee."[79]

Nothing favorable is ever said about Catholics or Episcopalians. Jews, Unitarians, Eastern Orthodox Christians, and other faith traditions are invisible throughout the text, as if they did not exist at all. "About 75 percent of the churches in the United States in the 1920s were fundamental in their beliefs," the reader is told.[80] This is a highly questionable assertion and not confirmed by the 1926 U.S. Census of Religious Bodies.

The author selects obscure figures for emulation in sidebars, rather than universally accepted figures of prominence in American history. Among those given extensive treatment are the evangelical missionaries William Taylor, Jedidiah Smith, Adoniram Judson, Townsend Harris, Jonathan Goble, and Jacob DeShazer.

The addition of the phrase "In God We Trust" to some U.S. coins during the 1860s is celebrated.

During the Civil War, the motto "In God We Trust" first appeared on United States coins. The man most responsible for the adoption of the motto was Secretary of the Treasury Salmon Chase, who sent the following memo to the director of the mint (the place where money is made): "No nation can be strong except in the strength of God, or safe except in His defense. The trust of our people in God should be declared on our national coins. You will cause a device to be prepared without unnecessary delay with a motto expressing in the fewest and tersest words possible this national recognition." The director of the mint composed several mottos and Chase chose "In God We Trust." Since that time, every coin issued by the United States has borne testimony to the nation's dependence on God. Day after day, as people work, shop, or play, they carry in their pockets and purses silent reminders of the greatness of God.[81]

This is false to the facts, however, since "In God We Trust" did not appear on all U.S. coins until well into the twentieth century, and not on the currency until after the Korean War.

Figures in secular history are praised more for their religious views than for their contributions to society. George Washington is praised for praying in the snow at Valley Forge,[82] for taking the Presidential oath of office on the Bible,[83] and for "stressing that a republic could work only if the people continued to do right according to God's laws."[84] Benjamin Franklin is lauded for his call for prayer at the Constitutional Convention.[85] Industrialist Cyrus McCormick is praised because "He used his money wisely and generously. Much of it he gave to good causes, including very large sums to the great evangelist D. L. Moody for the building of a YMCA building and a Christian Bible College."[86]

Confederate general Stonewall Jackson is seen as a Christian hero. "Stonewall Jackson had an outstanding Christian testimony that he shared with the men under him and around him. Church services were held in his tent whenever possible, and he passed out gospel tracts to his troops and encouraged them to pray faithfully and read their Bibles regularly."[87]

The denominational bias is seen again in the treatment accorded Theodore Roosevelt's upbringing. "Each morning, the family began the day by gathering around the Bible for family devotions. Teddy's father, knowing that a strong spiritual life was important to all young people, was one of the founders of the YMCA (Young Men's Christian Association)."[88] Never is it mentioned that Roosevelt attended the Dutch Reformed and Episcopal churches during his entire life, whereas McKinley's Methodism and Coolidge's Congregationalism are stressed.

Modern events are treated in a similarly fundamentalist manner. Chiang Kai-shek is called "a Christian and one of the greatest heroes of the twentieth century,"[89] while the foundation of Israel in 1948 is seen "as a major step in the unfolding of God's plan for the ages."[90]

In its treatment of Latin America, a bitter anti-Catholicism pervades the text. We are told that "the people of Central America need more than money: they need to hear the message of the gospel. Most people are Roman Catholic by religion, and it was not until the 1900s that Protestant missionaries began to take the story of Jesus Christ to the Central Americans. There are still many people who have not heard how to be saved."[91] For the Caribbean region, the reader is advised: "Since the days of Spanish rule, the majority of the people on many of the islands have been Roman Catholics. Often Catholicism is combined with voodooism and idol worship imported from Africa. The West Indies also has an impressive history of Protestant witness, however. Some of the first missionaries of modern times went there, and many Christians in the West Indies have endured great hardship to maintain a good Christian testimony."[92]

The section on South America is exceedingly prejudicial to the religious traditions of that continent. The author writes:

Before the Europeans came to Latin America, the Indians worshiped anything they could not understand—the sun, the moon, animals, trees, and water. The Spanish and Portuguese explorers were accompanied by Catholic priests who converted many Indians to Catholicism, often at the point of a sword. For many centuries, the Bible in South America has been almost an unknown book. The Indians often accepted the outward form of Catholicism and combined it with their own pagan worship.

Today, over 90 percent of all Latin Americans are Roman Catholics. The Catholic churches are huge, lavishly furnished buildings that contrast greatly with the poor houses of most of the people. One of the world's most expensive church buildings is in Salvador, Brazil's oldest city. The church auditorium is covered with pure gold.

The First Protestant missionary to South America, an Englishman named James Thomson, did not arrive until 1820. He started schools in Argentina, Uruguay, Chile, and Peru. The Bible was the main textbook. Thomson's schools were received warmly at first but were later persecuted by Catholic officials.

Other missionaries went through great hardships to get the Bible into the South American countries. One Argentinian Christian, Francisco Penzotti, went to Peru as a missionary, where he was imprisoned for selling Bibles.

South Americans who accepted Christ faced persecution from their friends and neighbors, but many stood firm in their new faith. By 1900, there was a Protestant witness in every country of South America.[93]

The author quotes W. Stanley Rycroft, *Religious Liberty in Latin America* (1942), who claims that the Catholic Church withholds the Bible from the people of Latin America and persecutes those who try to distribute it. Admitting that "some of this has changed today," she continues: "Many of the Latin American countries have constitutions that allow freedom of religion, but the spiritual and social hold of the old religion has not lessened. In five South American countries— Argentina, Bolivia, Colombia, Paraguay, and Peru—the Roman Catholic Church is the state church."[94] She fails to note that the vast majority of Latin American countries do not have an established church, and that *all* their constitutions provide for freedom of religion.

There is a distinct political bias conveyed to the students. While most historians of the presidency regard Jefferson, Lincoln, Jackson, Wilson, and the two Roosevelts as the greatest leaders in American political history, this volume has two peculiar favorites: James Garfield and Calvin Coolidge. Garfield, who was assassinated shortly after his inauguration, is admired because he was an evangelical believer and a lay preacher of the Disciples of Christ church. Two pages are devoted to Garfield, who is described as spiritual, gentle, well educated, and honest. Young Garfield, who had survived a boating accident, "knew God had saved his life for some purpose beyond that of being a canal hand."[95]

Calvin Coolidge is called "a man of good sense." The author extols this mediocre president in glowing terms:

> He was known for his scholarship, character, frugality, quiet humor, and good sense. He understood the people of the United States. He knew their strengths and their weaknesses, and he often said that the strength of the nation depended upon the character of the people.
>
> President Coolidge, who was from New England, greatly admired his Puritan ancestors. He spent a great deal of time studying their history and writings, and he also became a student of the Bible. From the Puritans and the Bible he learned the character traits that made generations of Americans great.[96]

A description of the First Amendment is not quite on target. The textbook says: "The United States was the first nation in the history of the world in which people were free to preach and practice any form of religion that does not interfere with morals or welfare of the community."[97] This is a less than adequate definition.

A conservative political bias pervades the geography section. For example, the widely admired central American nation of Costa Rica, which is considered by most scholars to be the best democracy south of the Rio Grande, is scathingly depicted in this book.

> For several years, Costa Rica has been a welfare state. This means that the government has taken the responsibility of caring for the people "from the cradle to the grave." Jobs, medical care, child care, and other services are provided by the government. This form of socialism has caused many problems in Costa Rica. Taxes keep going higher and higher, because the government services have to be paid for. People do not work hard, because they know the government will take care of them no matter what they do. The prices for goods have to go up to make up for the time and money wasted by lazy workers. Soon the poor people of the country cannot afford to buy necessities, and even the wealthier people have a hard time finding the goods they want. Socialism has brought poverty to this "rich coast."[98]

New World History and Geography similarly misteaches science. Evolution is denounced as a "false belief," and "modern anthropologists cannot always be trusted, because they often begin with false beliefs."[99] Frequent references are made to Noah's Ark, the Flood, and the Tower of Babel. The fundamentalist doctrine of "creationism" is repeatedly emphasized in both subtle and not so subtle ways.

These examples reveal a worldview clearly at odds with that of most Americans, including most Christians. While space does not permit more extensive examination of other textbooks, these representative samples reveal clearly the kind of education that prevails in many church-related schools in today's America. The point, of course, is not that religious institutions should be denied the freedom to teach as they please, but that schools that teach sectarian doctrines and slant material for purposes of denominational instruction or indoctrination should not be subsidized with public funds.

NOTES

1. Otto F. Kraushaar, *American Nonpublic Schools* (Baltimore, Md.: Johns Hopkins University Press, 1972), p. 22.

2. John L. McKenzie, *The Roman Catholic Church* (New York: Doubleday, 1971), pp. 294–95.

3. Neil J. McCluskey, S.J., *Catholic Viewpoint on Education* (New York: Image Books, 1962), pp. 74, 78.

4. Pius XI, encyclical letter *Divini Illius Magistri*, December 31, 1929: AAS 22 (1930).

5. *Lutheran Elementary Schools in Action*, Victoria C. Krause, ed. (St. Louis, Mo.: Concordia Press, 1963), p. 17.

6. Kraushaar, *American Nonpublic Schools*, pp. 104, 106.

7. *Issues of Aid to Nonpublic Schools* (Newton, Mass.: Center for Field Research and School Services, Boston College, 1971), pp. 16–23.

8. Sara E. Fisher and Rachel K. Stahl, *The Amish School* (Intercourse, Penn.: Good Books, 1986), p. 4.

9. Ibid., p. 88.

10. Ibid., p. 90, 91.

11. Ibid., p. 43.

12. Ibid., p. 40.

13. *Church & State* 35 (May 1982): 5.

14. *Church & State* 36 (March 1983): 18–19.

15. *Education Week*, May 22, 1991.

16. *Church & State* 40 (March 1987): 16–17.

17. 103 S Ct. 2017 (1983); *Church & State* 40 (May 1987): 3.

18. *Church & State* 36 (May 1983): 11.

19. Ibid., p. 12.

20. *Church & State* 37 (May 1984): 15.

21. Charles B. Hirsch, "Seventh-Day Adventist Education," *Church & State* 24 (April, 1971): 8.

22. Ibid., p. 9.

23. *Church & State* 23 (October 1970): 15.

24. Ibid.

25. Andrew M. Greeley, William C. McCready, and Kathleen McCourt, *Catholic Schools in a Declining Church* (Kansas City, Mo.: Sheed & Ward, 1976), p. 101.

26. Ibid.

27. Ibid.

28. Milo Brekke, *How Different Are People Who Attended Lutheran Schools?* (St. Louis, Mo.: Concordia Press, 1974), p. 34.

29. Ronald L. Johnstone, *The Effectiveness of Lutheran Elementary and Secondary Schools as Agents of Christian Education* (St. Louis, Mo.: Concordia Press, 1966).

30. John Diefenthaler, "Lutheran Schools in America," in *Religious Schooling in America*, James C. Carper and Thomas C. Hunt, eds. (Birmingham, Ala.: Religious Education Press, 1984), p. 53.

31. Ibid.

32. Ibid.

33. Alan Peshkin, *God's Choice: The Total World of a Fundamentalist Christian School* (Chicago: University of Chicago Press, 1986), p. 258.

34. Ibid., p. 259.

35. *Christian School Comment*, 1977, p. 1.

36. James C. Carper, "The Christian Day School," in Carper and Hunt, *Religious Schooling in America*, p. 111.

37. Ibid., p. 118.

38. Ibid.

39. Donald Opperval and Peter P. De Boer, "Calvinist Day Schools," in Carper and Hunt, *Religious Schooling in America*, p. 73.

40. Ibid.

41. Ibid., p. 74.

42. Ibid., p. 76.

43. George R. Knight, "Seventh-Day Adventist Education," in Carper and Hunt, *Religious Schooling in America*, p. 103.

44. Ibid.

45. Dean R. Esslinger, "Quakers in 19th-Century Baltimore," in *Maryland: Unity in Diversity*, A. Franklin Parks and John B. Wiseman, eds. (Dubuque, Iowa: Kendall Hunt, 1990), p. 57.

46. Lawrence A. Cremin, *American Education: The Colonial Experience* (New York: Harper and Row, 1970), p. 305.

47. Eduardo Rauch, "The Jewish Day School in America," in Carper and Hunt, *Religious Schooling in America*, p. 133. See also Walter I. Ackerman, "Jewish Education—For What?" *American Jewish Yearbook* 70 (1969): 17–18.

48. Ibid., p. 144.

49. Ibid., p. 145.

50. Ari L. Goldman, *The Search for God at Harvard* (New York: Random House, 1991), p. 103.

51. Ibid.

52. George R. LaNoue, "Religious Schools and Secular Subjects," *Harvard Educational Review* 32 (Summer 1962): 255–91.

53. John T. Pawlikowski, *Catechetics and Prejudice* (Mahwah, N.J.: Paulist Press, 1973), p. 9.

54. Michael J. McHugh and Charles Morris, *A Child's Story of America* (Arlington Heights, Ill.: Christian Liberty Press, 1989), p. 64.

55. Ibid., p. 70.

56. Ibid., p. 57.

57. Ibid., p. 19.

58. Ibid.

59. Ibid., p. 53.

60. Ibid., p. 85.

61. Ibid., p. 103.

62. Ibid., p. 55.
63. Ibid., p. 183.
64. Ibid., p. 186.
65. Ibid., pp. 262–63.
66. Ibid., p. 272.
67. Laurel Elizabeth Hicks, *New World History and Geography in Christian Perspective* (Pensacola, Fla.: Pensacola Christian College, 1982).
68. Ibid., p. 204.
69. Ibid., p. 208.
70. Ibid., p. 213.
71. Ibid., p. 210.
72. Ibid., p. 215.
73. Ibid., p. 219.
74. Ibid., p. 223.
75. Ibid., p. 224.
76. Ibid., pp. 304, 305.
77. Ibid., pp. 228–29.
78. Ibid., pp. 231–32.
79. Ibid., p. 259.
80. Ibid., p. 318.
81. Ibid., p. 279.
82. Ibid., p. 246.
83. Ibid., p. 252.
84. Ibid., p. 253.
85. Ibid., p. 251.
86. Ibid., p. 283.
87. Ibid., p. 275.
88. Ibid., p. 309.
89. Ibid., p. 331.
90. Ibid., p. 332.
91. Ibid., p. 140.
92. Ibid., p. 155.
93. Ibid., pp. 176–77.
94. Ibid., p. 177.
95. Ibid., pp. 286–87.
96. Ibid., p. 317.
97. Ibid., p. 252.
98. Ibid., p. 141.
99. Ibid.

3

Is Enrollment in Nonpublic Schools Booming?

Pertinent to the debate over public funding of nonpublic schools is the question of whether nonpublic enrollment has been expanding, as Jerry Falwell and other televangelists have widely claimed. Actual school enrollment figures, however, show that there has been no mass exodus from public education during the past twenty years. In fact, a higher percentage of students (89.3 percent) attended public elementary and secondary schools during the 1989–90 school year than did so during 1969–70, when 88.9 percent were enrolled in public schools.

The big change has been *within* the nonpublic sector, where Catholic schools have declined from 9.1 to 6 percent of total enrollment, a loss of one-third of the share. The non-Catholic sector, which includes Protestant, Jewish, and other religious schools as well as nonsectarian private schools, has more than doubled its share, from 2 percent to 4.7 percent of total enrollment.

Another change has been the decline in the total enrollment from 51.3 million students in 1969–70 to 45.4 million in 1989–90. This is a result of declining birth rates and the changing age composition of the U.S. population. (It is growing older rapidly, a change that will continue through the first decade of the next century, according to demographers.) Public school enrollment has declined from 45.6 million to 40.6 million pupils, while enrollment in private schools has declined from 5.7 million to 4.8 million (see Table 1). Total enrollment has declined in all but a few fast-growing states, such as Alaska, Arizona,

California, Colorado, Florida, Georgia, Idaho, Nevada, Oklahoma, South Carolina, Texas, Utah, and Wyoming. Enrollment is down by more than a million students in New York and by more than half a million in Illinois, Michigan, Ohio, and Pennsylvania.

TABLE 1

PUBLIC AND NONPUBLIC SCHOOL ENROLLMENT
TRENDS, 1969–70 TO 1989–90

	1969–70		1989–90	
Public	45,618,578	88.9%	40,537,285	89.3%
Catholic Nonpublic	4,688,059	9.1%	2,711,782	6.0%
Other Nonpublic	1,000,495	2.0%	2,135,224	4.7%
Total Nonpublic	5,688,554	11.1%	4,847,006	10.7%
Total	51,307,132		45,384,291	

Source: *Quality Education Data* (Denver 1990)

The decline in Catholic school enrollment is a major factor in the total educational picture. Over twenty years Catholic schools have lost almost two million students (from 4.7 million in 1969–70 to 2.7 million in 1989–90). The decline has affected *all fifty states* in terms of the percentage of total enrollment. The losses have been most severe in upper New England (Maine, New Hampshire, and Vermont) and in Idaho, Montana, and Wyoming. In these six states Catholic school enrollment has declined by more than half. In New Hampshire, for example, the Catholic school share fell from about 14 percent of all students to about 5 percent, and in Vermont, from about 8 percent to 3 percent. In three other western states (Arizona, Colorado, and Oregon) the decline has been almost 50 percent (see Table 2).

On the other hand, Catholic schools suffered only a modest decline in Alabama, Arkansas, Delaware, the District of Columbia, Kansas, Louisiana, Mississippi, Missouri, North Carolina, Oklahoma, South Carolina, and Tennessee. (In Utah the tiny Catholic school system also held up rather well.)

Catholic schools are proportionately strongest in Pennsylvania (12.8 percent of total enrollment) and Rhode Island (12.2 percent) in 1989–90. These were also the top two Catholic school states in 1969–70, although at that time roughly 17 percent of students in both states were attending Catholic schools.

Other states with strong Catholic school populations in 1989–90 include: Illinois (12.1 percent), New Jersey (11.7 percent), New York and Delaware (10.7 percent each), Louisiana (10.3 percent), Wisconsin (9.4 percent), Ohio and Massachusetts (9.3 percent), Connecticut (9.2 percent), Missouri (9.1 percent), and Nebraska (9 percent).

TABLE 2

CATHOLIC SCHOOL ENROLLMENT TRENDS,
1969–70 TO 1989–90, AS PERCENTAGE
OF TOTAL SCHOOL ENROLLMENT

State	1969–1970	1989–1990	State	1969–1970	1989–1990	State	1969–1970	1989–1990
Alab.	2.1%	1.7%	Ken.	8.6%	6.1%	N.D.	7.3%	5.2%
Alas.	1.2%	0.8%	La.	12.2%	10.3%	Oh.	12.0%	9.3%
Ariz.	5.1%	2.6%	Me.	5.1%	2.3%	Okla.	1.5%	1.2%
Ark.	1.9%	1.5%	Md.	9.8%	7.2%	Ore.	4.5%	2.3%
Calif.	6.2%	4.8%	Mass.	14.2%	9.3%	Penn.	17.2%	12.8%
Colo.	5.2%	2.7%	Mich.	9.8%	6.1%	R.I.	16.8%	12.2%
Conn.	12.2%	9.2%	Minn.	10.2%	6.7%	S.C.	1.2%	0.9%
Del.	11.6%	10.7%	Miss.	2.2%	1.9%	S.D.	5.9%	4.5%
D.C.	9.3%	8.7%	Mo.	10.5%	9.1%	Tenn.	2.0%	1.5%
Fla.	5.1%	3.6%	Mont.	5.6%	2.2%	Tex.	3.4%	2.1%
Geog.	1.3%	1.0%	Neb.	11.6%	9.0%	Utah	1.3%	0.9%
Haw.	N.A	6.4%	Nev.	3.4%	2.6%	Vt.	8.2%	3.1%
Id.	2.8%	1.0%	N.H.	13.8%	4.9%	Virg.	2.7%	1.9%
Ill.	15.2%	12.1%	N.J.	16.5%	11.7%	Wash.	4.3%	2.7%
Ind.	7.6%	5.2%	N.M.	4.0%	3.1%	W.V.	3.0%	1.9%
Iowa	9.5%	7.4%	N.Y.	16.3%	10.7%	Wisc.	14.2%	9.4%
Kans.	6.5%	5.6%	N.C.	1.0%	0.8%	Wyom.	2.9%	1.3%

Source: *Quality Education Data* (Denver 1990)

There is a moderate correlation between Catholic percentage of the state population and parochial school enrollment, though Delaware, Missouri, Ohio, and Nebraska are not heavily Catholic. Some Catholic strongholds, like New Hampshire, Vermont, and New Mexico, have low Catholic school enrollments.

Non-Catholic private schools have enjoyed an increase from 1 million to 2.1 million students during the past two decades. The growth pattern in this sector is overwhelmingly Southern. Nine of the top twelve private non-Catholic school states are in the South (Florida, Mississippi, South Carolina, Georgia, and Alabama) or the Chesapeake Bay region (Delaware, the District of Columbia, Maryland, and Virginia).

Somewhat surprisingly, Hawaii ranks first, with 11 percent of its students in Protestant or secular private schools. Hawaii is followed by Florida (8.4 percent), Delaware (8.3 percent), the District of Columbia (7.9 percent), Maryland (7.2 percent), Mississippi (6.9 percent), South Carolina (6.8 percent), Georgia (6.6 percent), New Hampshire (6.3 percent), Alabama (6.2 percent), and New York and Virginia (5.9 percent each) (see Table 3).

Compared to two decades ago, states in the Deep South have seen their private school enrollments increase from about 1 to 6 or 7 percent, a development probably stimulated by racial integration of public schools and some dissatisfaction with public education's cultural and religious policies on the part of fundamentalist and evangelical Protestants, who have moved aggressively into the education business (see Table 4). Still, it is difficult to analyze motivations. West Virginia, for example, was racked by dissension and violence into the mid-1970s over public school textbooks, but that state has experienced only a marginal increase in nonpublic enrollment. And the annual Gallup surveys of public attitudes toward education (sponsored by the Phi Delta Kappa educators organization) show a continued high acceptance of and satisfaction with public education by most parents in all regions of the country, with dissatisfaction concentrated among minority parents in inner cities.

There is also a long tradition of elite private education, including preparatory schools and military academies, in states like Delaware, Virginia, Maryland, New Hampshire, New York, and the District of Columbia, which may account for their relatively high private school enrollment figures.

TABLE 3

STATES WITH HIGHEST NON-CATHOLIC
NONPUBLIC (PROTESTANT, JEWISH, PRIVATE, ETC.)
SCHOOL ENROLLMENTS, 1989–90

1.	Hawaii	11.0%
2.	Florida	8.4%
3.	Delaware	8.3%
4.	District of Columbia	7.9%
5.	Maryland	7.2%
6.	Mississippi	6.9%
7.	South Carolina	6.8%
8.	Georgia	6.6%
9.	New Hampshire	6.3%
10.	Alabama	6.2%
11.	New York	5.9%
12.	Virginia	5.9%
National Average		4.7%

Source: *Quality Education Data* (Denver 1990)

There are strong regional patterns to educational preferences. The top ten states in terms of public school percentage of the school population are found in the West and the Border-South. Utah ranks first with 98.3 percent of its students in public schools. The Mormon factor is clearly evident here, since that state's dominant religious group has considerable influence in the public schools. Mormon influence is also strong in second-place Wyoming (97.4 percent) and Idaho (96.9 percent). Other states with strong public school predominance are Oklahoma (96.9 percent), West Virginia (96.5 percent), Arkansas (96.1 percent), Alaska (95.4 percent), Montana (95.4 percent), North Carolina (95 percent), and Nevada (94.9 percent). North Carolina and Arkansas are the only two Southern states that seem to have resisted the private Christian school movement (see Table 5).

TABLE 4

TRENDS IN NON-CATHOLIC,
NONPUBLIC SCHOOL ENROLLMENTS,
1969–70 TO 1989–90

State	1969–1970	%1969–1970	%1989–1990	State	1969–1970	%1969–1970	%1989–1990
Alab.	9,400	1.1%	6.2%	Mont.	6,566	3.4%	2.4%
Alas.	1,271	1.6%	3.8%	Neb.	8,960	2.3%	2.8%
Ariz.	8,607	1.9%	4.8%	Nev.	n.a.	n.a.	2.5%
Ark.	2,938	0.6%	2.4%	N.H.	7,171	3.9%	6.3%
Calif.	95,064	1.9%	5.6%	N.J.	6,835	0.4%	3.5%
Colo.	10,865	1.9%	3.5%	N.M.	10,271	3.4%	3.4%
Conn.	21,000	2.8%	5.2%	N.Y.	108,803	2.5%	5.9%
Del.	1,402	0.9%	8.3%	N.C.	8,869	0.7%	4.2%
D.C.	5,500	3.2%	7.9%	N.D.	5,598	3.4%	1.3%
Fla.	8,301	0.6%	8.4%	Oh.	11,585	0.4%	2.4%
Geog.	12,413	1.1%	6.6%	Okla.	7,313	1.2%	1.9%
Haw.	n.a	n.a.	11.0%	Ore.	8,715	1.7%	4.0%
Id.	2,946	1.6%	2.1%	Penn.	50,012	1.7%	4.8%
Ill.	67,857	2.4%	3.6%	R.I.	7,874	3.5%	3.0%
Ind.	24,621	2.5%	4.4%	S.C.	6,769	1.0%	6.8%
Iowa	19,242	2.6%	2.2%	S.D.	5,931	3.2%	2.3%
Kans.	9,438	1.7%	2.3%	Tenn.	14,332	1.6%	5.4%
Ken.	16,803	2.1%	2.3%	Tex.	46,414	1.6%	3.7%
La.	9,231	0.9%	4.8%	Utah	1,680	0.5%	0.8%
Me.	15,041	5.6%	4.8%	Vt.	6,179	5.3%	3.9%
Md.	25,300	2.5%	7.2%	Virg.	27,022	2.4%	5.9%
Mass.	37,912	2.7%	5.3%	Wash.	15,807	1.8%	4.7%
Mich.	76,259	3.1%	4.7%	W.V.	900	0.2%	1.6%

TABLE 4 (CONT.)

TRENDS IN NON-CATHOLIC,
NONPUBLIC SCHOOL ENROLLMENTS,
1969–70 TO 1989–90

State	1969–1970	%1969–1970	%1989–1990	State	1969–1970	%1969–1970	%1989–1990
Minn.	38,723	3.7%	3.7%	Wisc.	69,941	5.7%	5.8%
Miss.	6,374	1.1%	6.9%	Wyom.	1,002	1.1%	1.3%
Mo.	29,318	2.4%	3.6%				
			Total		1,000,495	2.0%	4.7%

Source: *Quality Education Data* (Denver 1990)

TABLE 5

STATES WITH HIGHEST PERCENTAGES OF
ENROLLMENT IN PUBLIC SCHOOLS, 1989–90

1.	Utah	98.3%
2.	Wyoming	97.4%
3.	Idaho	96.9%
4.	Oklahoma	96.9%
5.	West Virginia	96.5%
6.	Arkansas	96.1%
7.	Alaska	95.4%
8.	Montana	95.4%
9.	North Carolina	95.0%
10.	Nevada	94.9%
National Average		89.3%

Source: *Quality Education Data* (Denver 1990)

By contrast, the East and Midwest are areas where nonpublic schools have had more appeal. Delaware ranks first with 19 percent of its students attending all nonpublic (Catholic, Protestant, and non-religious) schools, followed by Pennsylvania (17.6 percent), Hawaii (17.4 percent), New York and the District of Columbia (16.6 percent). Illinois (15.7 percent), Rhode Island, Wisconsin, and New Jersey (all 15.2 percent), Louisiana (15.1 percent), Massachusetts (14.6 percent), and Connecticut and Maryland (14.4 percent each) also rank well above the national average (see Table 6).

TABLE 6

STATES WITH HIGHEST ENROLLMENTS IN ALL
NONPUBLIC SCHOOLS, 1989–90

1.	Delaware	19.0%
2.	Pennsylvania	17.6%
3.	Hawaii	17.4%
4.	New York	16.6%
5.	District of Columbia	16.6%
6.	Illinois	15.7%
7.	Rhode Island	15.2%
8.	Wisconsin	15.2%
9.	New Jersey	15.2%
10.	Louisiana	15.1%
11.	Massachusetts	14.6%
12.	Connecticut	14.4%
13.	Maryland	14.4%
National Average		10.7%

Source: *Quality Education Data* (Denver 1990)

We can note some distinct denominational/regional patterns. Seventh-Day Adventist schools are a significant part of the private school sector in Oregon and Washington. Reformed Church schools are strong in Michigan and Iowa, while Episcopal schools dot the countryside in Virginia and New Hampshire. Lutheran schools are particularly strong in Wisconsin. Baptist schools are burgeoning in enrollment in Tennessee and North Carolina, followed by Florida, Georgia, South Carolina, and Virginia.[1]

NOTE

1. W. Vance Grant and Thomas D. Snyder, *Digest of Education Statistics 1985–86* (Washington, D.C.: U.S. Government Printing Office, 1986), p. 72. See also the other primary and secondary school enrollment figures in the supplementary tables included in the Appendix to this volume.

4

Parochiaid in the States

The state parochiaid situation is complex and contradictory. It is complex because there are a myriad of indirect and even direct grant and aid programs benefitting church-related and other nonpublic schools in most states. It is contradictory because twenty-four states, while specifically prohibiting aid to sectarian educational institutions in their constitutions, do so anyway by legislation and statute. Indeed, forty-two states now provide some form of tax aid to nonpublic schools. (Those that do not are Alabama, Arkansas, Georgia, Oklahoma, Tennessee, Texas, Virginia, and Wyoming—largely Protestant states with low private school enrollments.)

Joseph Bryson and Samuel Houston describe the trend in their notable book, *The Supreme Court and Public Funds for Religious Schools*: "Although all state constitutions provide for church-state separation and the majority of constitutions make direct statements prohibiting financial aid to sectarian institutions, public tax dollars are in fact flowing to religious schools through a variety of statutory mandates. In 1981, forty states made public assistance available to religious schools. By 1983, the number had increased to forty-two. In many instances, appropriations are made directly to students rather than schools."[1]

TRANSPORTATION AID

The most common form of state aid comes in the form of transportation assistance, which occurs in twenty-seven states. The Bryson-Houston study indicates that these twenty-seven states "have statutes requiring school boards to provide transportation for religious-school students. Many of the statutes providing transportation for nonpublic students are designed in a delimiting fashion such as providing for no greater transportation service than approved for public-school students."[2]

As one might expect, New Jersey, the locale for the *Everson* decision of 1947, which began it all, provides cash stipends for transporting nonpublic school pupils. Parochial busing caused intense political division in Connecticut during the 1950s and in Wisconsin from the 1940s to the 1960s. In 1946 Wisconsin voters had turned down a busing proposal by a 55 to 45 percent margin, in which Protestants and Catholics were pitted against each other in a sharply divisive political combat. Twenty years later, a busing proposal was approved by the voters.

Bus transportation still results in legal conflict. In December 1982, the West Virginia Supreme Court ruled in *Janasiewicz* v. *Kanawha County Board of Education* that state law requires county public school boards to pay "adequate" transportation stipends to parochial school students or to establish special bus routes to serve them. This was an attempt to clarify differing patterns of aid provided by the counties, though the decision ignored an anomalous situation in Cabell County, where busing was provided to Catholic schools but not to those of other faiths.

State requirements vary widely. According to Richard E. Duffy, of the U.S. Catholic Conference's Department of Education, state busing programs are of three types: mandated, permissive, or narrowly permissive. He reported that many states mandate busing services for nonpublic schools at about the same level as for public schools, while some states merely permit local authorities to provide these services if they wish.

In states like Idaho and Maryland, local option prevails. Even within the same county or district, some public schools allow private school students to ride buses while others do not. In Idaho, some districts are allowing busing in apparent defiance of a 1971 state supreme court ruling forbidding the practice.

In some states, the extent of parochial busing has reached scandalous proportions. Pennsylvania's law requiring school districts to bus students to private schools located up to ten miles from township boundary lines was called "grossly unfair" by Millcreek School Board member Paul Quinn in 1982. Quinn wanted the board to deny transportation of four Millcreek Township students to Girard Christian Academy but his was the only dissenting vote. Urging exploration of a lawsuit "to bring the issue to the attention of legislators and taxpayers," Quinn observed that public school students had to attend the school nearest to their home while nonpublic school students were free to choose their school and still be bused at public expense. He charged that "some nonpublic students are bused across the township and then ten miles farther out." While some other board members agreed with Quinn's complaint, they admitted that nothing could be done about it.[3]

State school officials have lamented their helplessness in confronting the issue. The Chester County, Pennsylvania, Court of Common Pleas held in 1981 that the district was required to bus private school pupils even though the private school day ended at 5:30 P.M., several hours later than the public school day.

In Westmoreland County, Pennsylvania, WBCW-Radio talk show host Al Calisti reported that a local public had been required to provide a private taxi service at $48 per day, or more than $17,000 per school year, for two private school pupils.

In Ohio, the Perrysburg Board of Education refused to transport parochial pupils far outside the district to West Toledo because of the exorbitant costs involved. (The cost to bus students to Notre Dame School was $1,229 per pupil, while busing a student to the average public school cost only about $104.) But when parochial school parents sued the district to force compliance, a Wood County court ordered the district to provide taxi services. On December 13, 1982, the Ohio State Board of Education issued a "determination" upholding the local school board.

A certain amount of church-state entanglement seems to occur when public and nonpublic schools try to work out formulas for distribution of funds. Louisiana, for example, reimburses parents up to $375 per year for school transportation costs. About 95 percent of the $6.5 million annual appropriations go to parochial school patrons. Parents of eligible students file forms with their local private school which in turn sends the forms to the local public school authority. The names are sent to the state education department, and checks are issued each August. In the Archdiocese of New Orleans, however, applications for the parochial busing stipend are processed by the church and then delivered to the state authorities in Baton Rouge. The archdiocese receives state funds to process the paperwork. The Louisiana practice, however, is under court challenge, and private school interests are reportedly worried about losing their bounteous provisions.

In Kentucky a state constitutional prohibition on direct expenditures of funds for nonpublic school transportation has been circumvented in clever ways. Henderson County Attorney William Markwell worked out an agreement by which the county will pay 88 percent of busing costs while the local Catholic school system pays only 12 percent.

In 1983 Americans for Religious Liberty (ARL) estimated that the total annual cost to taxpayers of busing nonpublic students for the 1980–81 school year was $585 million. While hard cost figures are hard to come by, reasonable estimates can be extrapolated from publicly available data. Of the five million students then in nonpublic schools, 3.1 million were in states that provide full transportation services for their schools. Since 57 percent of public school students were transported at an average annual cost of $176 per year (1980–81), the nonpublic school transportation costs were at least $311 million annually. However, nonpublic schools tend to serve more scattered constituencies and their attendance areas usually do not coincide with those of public schools, so nonpublic school transportation costs more per student—44 percent more in New Jersey, 63 percent more in New York, and 156 percent more in the Washington, D.C., metropolitan area. Averaging these differentials, ARL estimated $585 million as the probable annual cost to taxpayers for nonpublic school transportation in the "full service" states. In addition, partial transportation services in nine other states cost, by conservative estimate, another $22.5 million.[4] If transportation costs have kept up with the rate of inflation, then nonpublic transportation costs were exceeding $1 billion annually by 1990–91.

OTHER AID

Textbooks

Seventeen states "lend"* textbooks to nonpublic schools or their students. Since 1980, several states (California, Colorado, Iowa, Maine, Minnesota, and New Hampshire) have expanded their textbook aid to include media and instructional materials. Textbooks are supposed to be nonsectarian and on approved state textbook lists. Evidence from some states, especially Louisiana, however, has shown that state authorities often look the other way when church schools overload book selections with denominationally slanted material.

ARL has estimated that nonpublic school textbook loans in 1980–81 cost taxpayers $42.5 million, based on the New York–New Jersey average of $15 per student per year. Inflation alone would have raised that figure to at least $75 million by 1990–91.

Health Care and Lunch Programs

Falling under the general category of "child benefits" are aid for health services and school lunch programs for needy students. Thirteen states provide the former and nine states, the latter. Some of these statutes are "enabling" legislation for federal programs, while others are separate state programs. These services can be broad and include speech and hearing diagnostic services, psychological services, and therapeutic speech programs. Extensive "auxiliary services" diagnostic and remedial programs in Ohio, Pennsylvania, New Jersey, and New York were costing taxpayers about $138 million per year in the early 1980s, according to the ARL study.[5]

Driver Education

Fourteen states provide for state-funded driver education courses at private school locations, or allow nonpublic school students to take the courses on public high school campuses.

---

*"Lending" textbooks is generally a euphemism for giving them outright. A loaned textbook seldom survives more than two years' use.

"Shared Time"

Then there is the hybrid strategem called "shared time," which is available in Colorado, Illinois, Iowa, Minnesota, New Hampshire, and Pennsylvania. Shared time involves the sending of nonpublic students to public schools for specific courses that are unavailable in the nonpublic school. This is a form of "cooperation" that primarily aids the private school by having the public schools teach nonpublic students those subjects which are not considered "core" to the nonpublic school's religious mission. There are no accurate statistics available to show the extent and cost of "shared time" parochiaid. (Getting good statistics on parochiaid has always been a problem because the U.S. Department of Education has always buried state and federal expenditures for nonpublic schools in the public education figures, thus concealing the extent of tax aid for sectarian schools and overreporting the amount of tax support going to public schools.)

An interesting variation on the "shared time" plan is "reversed shared time," a scheme operating in Grand Rapids, Michigan, for several years until the U.S. Supreme Court ruled it unconstitutional in 1985 in *Grand Rapids School District* v. *Ball.*[6] Under a "reversed shared time" plan, a public school district leases or rents classrooms in a parochial school and staffs them with public school teachers. The students involved thus take some regular parochial school classes, such as religion or social studies, and some public school classes, such as mathematics or science, in the same parochial school building and setting. The nonpublic school students, then, would hardly be aware that a good part of their education was coming from public funds. "Reversed shared time" was the practical equivalent of handing a check drawn from the public treasury over to the treasury of the church operating the private school.

Some Additional Revenues

Bryson and Houston have tracked additional types of parochiaid which are nothing if not ingenious. New York, Ohio, Rhode Island, and Louisiana reimburse nonpublic schools for state-required record keeping. Maryland allows nonpublic schools access to closed circuit educational television programs operated for public schools. Arizona allows exemption from motor vehicle weight fees for nonpublic school transportation. Nevada gives surplus federal property to nonpublic schools.[7]

TABLE 7

STATE ASSISTANCE TO RELIGIOUS
ELEMENTARY AND SECONDARY SCHOOLS

State	Transportation	Textbooks and/or Instructional Materials	Lunches	Health Services and/or Auxiliary Services	Shared Time	Driver Education	Other Direct Aid	Miscellaneous
Ark.	X		X					X
Ariz.				X			X	X
Calif.	X	X	X			X		X
Colo.		X			X			
Conn.	X	X	X	X		X	X	X
Del.	X					X		
Fla.						X		X
Haw.				X		X		
Id.						X		
Ill.	X		X		X	X		
Ind.	X							
Iowa	X	X	X	X	X	X		X
Kans.				X				
Ken.	X				X			
La.	X	X	X			X	X	X
Me.	X	X		X				
Md.	X			X				X
Mass.	X	X		X				
Mich.	X			X		X		
Minn.	X	X		X	X	X		
Miss.		X		X		X	X	
Mo.			X					
Mont.	X							

(continued on next page)

TABLE 7 (CONT.)

STATE ASSISTANCE TO RELIGIOUS
ELEMENTARY AND SECONDARY SCHOOLS

State	Transpor-tation	Textbooks and/or Instruc-tional Materials	Lunches	Health Services and/or Auxiliary Services	Shared Time	Driver Education	Other Direct Aid	Miscel-laneous
Neb.	X							
Nev.	X		X					X
N.H.	X	X	X	X	X	X		X
N.J.	X	X	X	X				X
N.M.		X						
N.Y.	X	X		X			X	
N.C.								X
N.D.	X							
Oh.	X	X		X		X	X	X
Ore.	X		X			X		
Penn.	X	X	X	X	X	X	X	
R.I.	X	X	X		X		X	
S.C.							X	
S.D.		X				X		
Utah						X		
Vt.						X	X	
Wash.					X			
W.V.	X	X						
Wisc.	X					X		

Source: Bryson and Houston, *The Supreme Court and Public Funds for Religious Schools* (1990), p. 63.

CONCLUSION

As this overview indicates, the parochiaiders have been extraordinarily clever and successful in circumventing both state constitutions and federal court rulings to achieve many of their objectives. The trend has been very much in their favor, leading Bryson and Houston to conclude: "From 1980 to 1986, the trend was to expand legislative increments providing more and more assistance to religious schools. The latter four years gave private schools an even firmer grasp on public purse strings."[8]

As can be seen from Table 7 showing state programs, certain states have enacted more parochiaid programs than others. The worst offenders are Connecticut, Iowa, New Hampshire, and Pennsylvania, followed by Ohio and Louisiana. These states have had aggressive parochiaid lobbies, compliant legislatures, and above-average private school populations. But other states with similar political cultures, e.g., Massachusetts and Michigan, have not been so generous.

NOTES

1. Joseph Bryson and Samuel Houston, *The Supreme Court and Public Funds for Religious Schools* (Jefferson, N.C.: McFarland & Co., 1990), p. 54.

2. Ibid., p. 60.

3. "Transportation Parochiaid Rolls Onward," *Church & State* 36 (February, 1983): 9–10.

4. *Americans for Religious Liberty Newsletter*, No. 10 (Fall 1983): 4.

5. Ibid.

6. 473 US 373.

7. Bryson and Houston, *The Supreme Court and Public Funds for Religious Schools*, p. 62.

8. Ibid., p. 64.

5

The People Speak:
The Parochiaid Referenda, 1966–1990

Public opinion polls often show a degree of popular confusion over the issue of tax support for nonpublic schools, due generally to pollsters' use of confusing or misleading questions; moreover, court decisions have upheld the church-state separation principle with something less than consistency. But the decisions of voters in more than a dozen states from coast to coast during the past quarter-century do show a consistent pattern: overwhelming support for the principle of separation as it applies to the financing of education.

Since 1966, eighteen referendum elections in thirteen states have resulted in seventeen wins and only one loss for church-state separation in education. Time after time in state after state voters have rejected schemes to divert public funds to religious schools or to weaken state constitutional prohibitions on state aid to sectarian institutions. Indeed, the pattern is so clear and decisive that political observers and politicians should take note of this history.

The modern church-state referendum story begins in Nebraska in 1966.

HISTORY

1966: Nebraska

A proposed amendment to the state constitution to allow tax funds to be used to provide bus service for parochial schools was rejected by the state's voters 57 percent to 43 percent.

1967: New York

When New Yorkers voted in 1965 to approve the calling of a state constitutional convention, a predominantly Catholic parochiaid lobby group called Citizens for Educational Freedom (CEF) saw its chance. In a quiet but intense campaign, CEF won a majority of the delegate seats at the convention by concentrating votes on the minority of candidates favoring removal of the anti-parochiaid section of the state constitution. The "stacked deck" convention did what CEF wanted. But then their luck ran out.

Religious, educational, parent, labor, and other groups formed the Committee for Public Education and Religious Liberty (PEARL) to counter the threat to church-state separation. In the November 1967 constitutional ratification election, New Yorkers voted down the entire proposed new state constitution 72.5 percent to 27.5 percent. Since the rest of the proposed constitution was generally unobjectionable, its defeat may fairly be ascribed to the single overriding issue—parochiaid.

The New York vote was also significant because the parochiaiders spent a reported $2 million to win the referendum, compared to only about $50 thousand by the defenders of church-state separation.

Every county rejected the constitution. Protestant rural areas were four to one against it, as were Jewish strongholds. But even Catholic voters were opposed, despite Cardinal Francis Spellman's very visible campaigning in the measure's favor.[1]

1970: Michigan

Michigan's legislature proved increasingly compliant to the demands of parochiaiders in the late 1960s. So a coalition of defenders of church-state separation initiated by petition a proposed amendment to the state constitution to make even more explicit the already existing prohibition of parochiaid. When the November votes were counted, the church-state separation amendment had won 57 percent to 43 percent. The outcome caught pollsters, editorialists, and local politicians by surprise. Expenditures favored the parochiaid side, and polls had failed to capture voter sentiment accurately.

Parochiaid carried in only thirteen of Michigan's 83 counties. An examination of these thirteen counties indicates that eight are predominantly Roman Catholic, while four of the other five counties have substantial Catholic minorities. However, of the five heaviest counties for parochiaid, only two are predominantly Catholic. One county is half Catholic, half Lutheran. The other two are heavily Christian Reformed (Dutch Reformed), a church that operates many parochial schools. Another significant point is that other predominantly Catholic counties voted against parochiaid. Only 51 percent of the nineteen most heavily Catholic counties, taken as a whole, voted for parochiaid, only 8 percent higher than the statewide average.

Of the 70 counties opposing parochiaid, 11 cast over 70 percent of their votes against it. Several of these counties are referred to as "Yankee-Protestant counties" because their original inhabitants came from the New England states whose leading churches are Methodist, United Church of Christ, Baptist, and Disciples of Christ. University counties voted two to one against parochiaid.

1970: Nebraska

In Nebraska, CEF and the Catholic hierarchy got the legislature to initiate a proposed state constitutional amendment to authorize a tuition reimbursement plan. On election day the amendment was defeated 57 percent to 43 percent. Parochiaid carried in only 11 of the state's 93 counties. Seven of these are predominantly Roman Catholic, while three are predominantly Lutheran but have large Catholic minorities. Of Nebraska's eight predominantly Catholic counties, seven voted for parochiaid with an aggregate support of 56 percent. Of the 82 counties that voted against parochiaid, 10 cast majorities of better than 70 percent. These counties are either Lutheran or Methodist. In none of these counties is there any significant Catholic population.

1972: Idaho

Idaho voters rejected a proposed constitutional amendment to allow transportation aid for parochial schools by 57 percent to 43 percent.

Only three of Idaho's 44 counties voted for parochiaid. Of them two are predominantly Catholic, while the third has a Mormon majority. Of the state's five Roman Catholic counties, only two voted for parochiaid and only 48 percent of the aggregate vote favored it. Most of the state's counties are predominantly Mormon. The six completely Mormon counties voted two to one against parochiaid.

Even the political right wing failed to support the Idaho measure. In four of the state's counties—Fremont, Jefferson, Lemhi, and Madison—the American Party's presidential candidate, John Schmitz, actually ran ahead of Democrat George McGovern in 1972. Schmitz received 28 percent of the vote cast in Jefferson County and 17 percent in Madison County. These counties voted against parochiaid by an aggregate of more than 70 percent.

1972: Maryland

In 1971 the Maryland legislature, after several years of defeat for parochiaiders, passed a bill to provide $12 million per year to parochial schools under a complex voucher plan. Opposing groups gathered enough voters' signatures to put the bill to a referendum in November 1972. Marylanders then voted the bill down 55 percent to 45 percent.

Outside of Baltimore City, only two of the 23 counties—predominantly Catholic Charles and St. Mary's Counties in southern Maryland—favored the voucher and auxiliary services proposal. The Catholic stronghold of Emmitsburg in Frederick County supported the measure 70 percent to 30 percent. Maryland has a number of solidly Methodist counties. All opposed parochiaid. The seven strongest Methodist counties on the Eastern Shore opposed parochiaid by margins ranging from 63 percent to 79 percent. The Methodist opposition to parochiaid was a major factor in the state's rejection of the proposal.

In western Maryland three counties are historically German-American, and a majority of church members are either Lutheran, Reformed, or Brethren. These counties voted 62–67 percent against the measure. Garrett, the state's banner Republican county, which has *never* gone Democratic in presidential elections, voted two to one against parochiaid.

Precinct data from Montgomery County and Baltimore City are quite revealing. In Montgomery County almost every precinct opposed parochiaid, but in two particular areas the vote was better than two to one in opposition. The Jewish vote in Rosemary Hills and south Silver Spring, which voted heavily for McGovern in the 1972 election, was strongly against parochiaid. The conservative Protestant vote in some of the county's rural areas, such as Clarksburg and Poolesville (the most pro-Nixon precincts in the county), also voted heavily against parochiaid.

In Baltimore City, Jewish and liberal pro-McGovern areas voted most heavily against parochiaid, as did the majority of blacks. The Jewish precincts opposed parochiaid by about 65–35 percent. Black precincts cast 58 percent of their votes against parochiaid but were quite erratic. A number of black ghetto precincts voted for parochiaid, but those in more middle-class areas were against it. The black turnout was also erratic. Only 36.8 percent of those who voted in the presidential race cast votes on the parochiaid referendum.

Over 69 percent of the Catholic vote in East Baltimore's Polish enclaves was for parochiaid, with over 77 percent in some precincts. An Italian precinct voted 68 percent in favor. A Catholic middle-class suburb voted about 65 percent for the measure. The Catholic voter turnout on the referendum exceeded that of all other groups, perhaps because they felt most directly affected by the measure. (One interesting result came in blue-collar Catholic Dundalk, where voters narrowly rejected the proposal.)

1972: Oregon

Oregon voters were presented by the legislature with a proposed amendment to replace a strong anti-parochiaid state constitutional provision with a weaker, vaguer one, patterned after the provision voted down in New York just five years earlier. Oregonians defeated the measure 69 percent to 39 percent, a fact which the state's junior Republican senator, Robert Packwood, seemed to have forgotten during the 1977–1978 congressional battles over tuition tax credit parochiaid.

All 36 of Oregon's counties voted against parochiaid, and in only one county was it even close. Parochiaid ran slightly better in Portland and its suburbs than elsewhere. Since Oregon has a low percentage of church members, this secular orientation undoubtedly contributed to the defeat of the parochiaid measure. Oregon is also very much a WASP state: it does not have large numbers of minorities or ethnic groups.

1974: Maryland

Less than two years after their 1972 electoral defeat, Maryland parochiaiders got the legislature to enact another bill, this time for $9.7 million per year for books, equipment, supplies, and transportation for parochial schools. Once again groups concerned with defending church-state separation and public education petitioned the bill to a referendum. After an acrimonious campaign, Maryland voters defeated the new parochiaid bill 57 percent to 43 percent.

Pro-parochiaid forces were dealt a heavier defeat than in 1972. Parochiaid was defeated by greater margins than before in 17 of the state's 24 jurisdictions, while receiving a slightly higher vote in seven of them. The greater Baltimore area alone gave parochiaid a slightly higher vote than in 1972 while the Washington, D.C., suburbs voted against parochiaid by a 4 percent greater margin.

The state's heavily Methodist Eastern Shore counties turned in even heftier majorities than in 1972, with votes ranging from 75 percent to 83 percent against the proposal. Some of the more stunning swings against parochiaid came in several western Maryland counties, which historically are mixed religiously but have a predominance of Lutherans. In Washington County, for example, parochiaid was defeated by 78 percent compared to 67 percent in the previous referendum. In Allegany, Carroll, and Garrett Counties, the defeat was 4 to 6 percent greater than before. The polarization between Catholics and non-Catholics on this issue seemed to have increased.

Jewish voters turned in strong majorities against the measure, though the pattern was mixed. The Jewish precincts in Silver Spring increased from 70 percent to 73 percent against, while the Jewish ward in Baltimore City declined from 65 percent to 60 percent. The more rural Protestant precincts in several counties tended to be heavily against parochiaid. University students in two precincts also voted against the measure. The same majority of 57 percent was recorded in the Johns Hopkins University precinct in Baltimore, while the University of Maryland precinct increased from 56 percent to 62 percent opposed.

The state's black voters showed the biggest swing against the parochiaid measure. In two precincts in Prince George County (suburban Washington) opposition increased by almost 11 percent, as 65 percent of the voters rejected parochiaid. In nine key black precincts in Baltimore City, opposition increased from 65 percent to 72 percent.

Other than Roman Catholic areas, the only precincts that showed greater support for parochiaid were several blue-collar Protestant precincts in Baltimore City, where opposition to public school busing had been running high. These precincts, in fact, turned in a much larger increase in parochiaid support than the Catholic areas.

1975: Washington State

The next state to face a referendum on parochiaid was Washington. The legislature, responding to pressure both from parochial schools and denominational colleges, proposed a state constitutional amendment to allow unlimited tax aid to denominational private education. The state's voters defeated the amendment 60.5 percent to 39.5 percent.

The parochiaid measure was defeated in all the state's 39 counties, in seven counties by more than 70 percent of the voters. In only five counties did the margin of victory drop to between 55 and 60 percent.

The state's four urban-suburban counties voted against parochiaid by 58–42 percent. The small town and rural counties voted no by 65–35 percent. The three most heavily Republican counties voted 65 percent against the measure, while the three heaviest Democratic counties voted 63 percent against. It appears that voter turnout affected the size of the defeat for the measure. Washington has always had a remarkably vigorous electorate. Of the state's registered voters, 55 percent turned out for this off-year election, which also included other important referendum questions. The three counties that had the highest turnout voted 64 percent against the measure while the three counties having the lowest turnout voted 59 percent against parochiaid.

Religious influences on the election were minimal. Washington, like Oregon and California, has a low percentage of residents who are church members. About one-third of the state's church members are Roman Catholic, but only about one in nine of the state's total population is Roman Catholic. An analysis of the vote shows a modest correlation between Catholic population and the vote in this referendum. Spokane, the state's most heavily Catholic county, cast a higher than average vote in favor of the measure. On the other hand, two of the six counties that voted most heavily against parochiaid also have large Catholic populations.

1976: Alaska

In November Alaska voters turned down a proposed amendment to allow unlimited state aid to private denominational schools and colleges. The vote was 54 percent to 46 percent.

1976: Missouri

Parochiaid advocates in Missouri, long a battleground on the issue, initiated by petition a proposed state constitutional amendment to authorize $10 million in state aid in the form of transportation, textbooks, and auxiliary services. The parochiaiders induced Governor Christopher Bond to schedule the ratification referendum on August 3, in the hope that public school teachers and parents would be unable to organize during the summer to defeat the measure. The strategy failed. On August 3 Missourians defeated the amendment 60 percent to 40 percent.

Missouri's referendum produced the tenth straight defeat in as many years for the advocates of government aid to nonpublic schools. Missouri, which probably has the strictest constitutional prohibition on government assistance to religion, faced a referendum after Roman Catholic and Missouri Synod Lutheran school patrons gathered enough petitions to force the issue to a vote.

From the outset observers worried about a Baptist-Catholic clash in a state where religious antagonisms are an established political fact. Both proponents and opponents of Constitutional Amendment Number 7 denied that sectarianism would determine the level of debate or the ultimate outcome. Instinctively, however, Baptists and Catholics, the state's dominant religions, lined up on opposite sides of the fence. The pro-parochiaid campaign was quiet, with Catholic newspapers doing little more than urge a yes vote. The statewide Baptist paper

Word and Way gave the issue tremendous prominence, calling it "the most crucial issue of the decade." Baptists and many other Protestants saw the election as a showdown on religious liberty and plunged into the fray with great élan.

The results were decisive. By a 60–40 percent margin, voters rejected the constitutional change. The vote was much heavier than had been anticipated. The pro-parochiaid Fairness in Education executive director, Jerome R. Porath, accurately forecast 450,000 yes votes, but admitted that his group had underestimated the volume of opposition feeling.[2]

Once again religious affiliation shaped the voters' response to this issue. More than in any other state, the Missouri electorate divided along religious lines. The two heaviest Catholic counties voted 79 percent and 72 percent in favor. The four overwhelmingly Baptist counties said no, with margins ranging from 74 percent to 82 percent. The Catholic character of Greater St. Louis and Kansas City resulted in a 50,000-vote majority for the proposition there, but in the solidly Protestant rural and small-town areas the measure lost by 275,000 votes. Boone County, containing the University of Missouri, voted 64 percent against. A "Yankee Protestant" and Republican county voted no by a margin of four to one. A German Protestant Republican stronghold voted 68 percent no, while a banner Democratic county in "Mark Twain country," the only county outside of St. Louis to back George McGovern, voted 64 percent against.

A survey conducted on election day among 900 voters in Boone County revealed the tremendous cleavage. Almost 80 percent of the Catholics voted yes, while 75 percent of the Baptists voted no.[3] The survey also found that 14 percent of the voters were confused by the ballot wording. Apparently 11 percent who opposed parochiaid voted for the amendment, while 3 percent who favored it voted no.

Baptist leaders hailed the vote as a reaffirmation of religious liberty. Catholics were disappointed, even angry, at the outcome. The *St. Louis Review* (August 6, 1976) claimed that "ignorance and bigotry" were accountable for the defeat of this proposal. It accused opponents of carrying on a "vicious campaign stirring up anti-Catholic bias." Protestant clergymen, it said, "were leaders in fanning the flames of prejudice." The paper ended with a warning for the future: "Victims of prejudice often band together for redress of grievances. Those who made this election into a religious controversy may have sparked such a reaction." Yet the fact is that the controversy was precipitated by the efforts of Catholic and Missouri Synod Lutheran school patrons to impose some of the costs of denominational schools on all taxpayers.

1978: Michigan

The next referendum on parochiaid took place in Michigan. Parochial school interests went all out, initiating by petition a proposed constitutional amendment to provide parochial, private, and public schools with equal support under an unspecified voucher plan. The parochiaid amendment even included a clause abolishing property taxes for education! But Michigan voters were not giving in, and on November 7th voters buried the amendment in a 74 percent to 26 percent landslide.

1981: District of Columbia

Washington, D.C., voters went to the polls in record numbers on November 7 to deal the tuition tax credit parochiaid plan a crushing defeat. The final vote count on Initiative 7 was 73,829 to 8,904, an 89–11 percent drubbing that had profound effects on the campaign to get Congress to enact a national tuition tax credit plan.

Over 30 percent of the District of Columbia's registered voters turned out to vote, more than double the average percentage in off-year elections. The 8,904 voters in favor of the plan amounted to only a third of the number of voters who had initially signed petitions the previous summer to put the controversial measure on the ballot.

The Initiative 7 parochiaid plan was petitioned onto the ballot by the D.C. Committee for Improved Education, an affiliate of the National Taxpayers Union (NTU), which put up 99 percent of the estimated $135,000 spent in putting the measure on the ballot and campaigning for its passage.* (The NTU has also been the main force behind a campaign to have state legislatures force Congress to call a national constitutional convention, the first since 1787. Although the ostensible purpose of the convention would be to amend the Constitution to require a balanced federal budget, constitutional authori-

---

*The NTU tried unsuccessfully to get a similar proposal, a state constitutional amendment, onto the ballot in California in 1979.

ties generally agree that, like the 1787 convention, a new convention could not be limited to a single amendment, but could very well consider amendments that might conceivably tear the heart out of the Bill of Rights.)

Under the Initiative 7 plan, *each* D.C. resident taxpayer, including businesses, could have gotten a 100 percent credit against the D.C. income tax of up to $1,200 for paying for each child's "qualified education expenses," such as tuition, fees, transportation, uniforms, books, materials, and incidentals. The tax credit would have applied to school expenses for D.C. children attending parochial or private schools in the District of Columbia, in neighboring Maryland or Virginia, or anywhere else in the world.

Moreover, the language of the defeated bill would not have limited the tax credit to $1,200 per student, but would have allowed households of more than one taxpayer to receive up to $1,200 each in education tax credits for a single student. Thus, an employed couple could each have gotten a $1,200 credit for a single child's parochial or private school expenses, and their employers could each get a $1,200 credit against D.C. taxes for contributing to the couple's child's schools expenses, for a total D.C. tax expenditure of $4,800.

Estimates of the costs to D.C. taxpayers of the Initiative 7 parochiaid plan ranged from $25 million to $75 million annually, depending upon how many taxpayers would have been able to take advantage of it. The full $1,200 per taxpayer credit would have gone only to taxpayers earning over $21,500 per year, thus benefitting to the maximum only a minority of D.C. residents.

Most of the opposition to Initiative 7 was coordinated by two separate but cooperating coalitions, the D.C. Coalition Against Tuition Tax Credits and the D.C. Coalition for Public Education. Working within and in league with the two anti-parochiaid coalitions were teacher and parent organizations, labor unions, the Council of Churches and the Jewish Community Council of Greater Washington, the D.C. Baptist Convention, the National Conference of Christians and Jews, the League of Women Voters, the ACLU, the National Urban League and the NAACP, the D.C. Federation of Civic Associations, the D.C. City Council and Board of Education, Mayor Marion Barry, the D.C. Chamber of Commerce and the Board of Trade, and other groups.

While Catholic archdiocesan school board president Terence

Scanlon and some Catholic priests and laymen worked to pass the measure, Archibishop James A. Hickey publicly took a neutral stance and ordered Catholic parish and school officials to remain neutral as well. Hickey noted that more than half of the Catholic children in Washington attend public schools. "I am concerned for the children in all our schools," Hickey said.

Other parochial and private school officials in the District either remained neutral or opposed the plan. Many of them said that Initiative 7 would harm the public schools and have adverse effects on the city's already strained budget.

1982: California

By a 61–39 percent margin, California residents turned down Proposition 9, an amendment that would have allowed a publicly financed program of textbook aid to parochial and other private schools. The $5 million program was in operation until 1981 when the State Supreme Court held that it violated the state constitution's prohibition of aid to church education.

At least ten of the state's twelve Roman Catholic dioceses "lent" large sums of money to the committee pushing Proposition 9. The Catholic parochial school system would have been by far the largest beneficiary of the textbook aid program.

The *National Catholic Reporter* revealed that diocesan spending included $100,000 from Los Angeles; $45,410 from San Francisco; $38,110 from Oakland; $29,405 from San Jose; $28,000 from Sacramento; $25,000 from San Diego; $20,000 from San Bernardino; $12,670 from Stockton; $10,500 from Santa Rosa; and $10,000 from Monterey. Dr. Joseph McElligott, director of education for the California Catholic Conference, told the *Reporter* that the loans were to be repaid "to some extent."

These large contributions paid for various campaign activities, including sophisticated statewide television advertising. The ads featured veteran actress Helen Hayes, a New York resident, urging Californians to "vote for books for children." The campaign was also supported by a full-page ad in the *Los Angeles Times* by the local Catholic archdiocese urging a yes vote on the proposition.

Both candidates for governor and both candidates for state superintendent of public instruction, as well as several state newspapers, including both San Francisco dailies, also endorsed the ballot measure. The *Los Angeles Times* and the *Herald-Examiner* came out against the measure, however.

The opposition to Proposition 9, including the public school community, civil liberties groups, and many Jewish and Protestant religious organizations, fought the measure with only volunteer efforts. The "No on Nine" committee spent less than $10,000, according to local estimates. A Mervin Field poll conducted on election day affirmed that voters opposed the parochiaid plan because they thought private schools' textbooks should not be subsidized by the taxpayers.

1982: Massachusetts

The citizens of Massachusetts voted 62–38 percent against Question 1, which would have allowed "aid, materials, or services" to pupils in private schools. The proposed state constitutional amendment was intended to replace the existing strong anti-parochiaid section and allow the legislature to start programs of textbook aid and other forms of assistance to nonpublic schools by funneling the money through students.

Question 1 appeared likely to pass. The state's Catholic bishops issued a pastoral letter to be read in all parishes urging Catholics to vote for the measure (Massachusetts is 52 percent Catholic, the second most Catholic state in the union). In addition, public schools in Boston and some other areas of the state had been beset with problems.

A coalition of public-school, civil liberties, and Jewish and Protestant religious groups, similar to the one in California, managed to get the "No on One" message out to the voters.

A combination of factors prompted the measure's defeat, including concern that funds would be diverted from the already underfunded public schools to private schools, the possibility of a tax increase to pay for new private school programs, and support for the principle of church-state separation.

Voters of all faiths rejected the proposal.

1986: Massachusetts

Parochiaid advocates once again tried to weaken the Bay State's strict constitutional prohibition against church-state entanglement. They hoped to open the door to such "indirect" programs as vouchers, tax credits, textbook loans, and auxiliary services. Question 2 on the ballot was designed to accomplish their purposes, and a Committee for Educational Equality was set up to shepherd the campaign.

Cardinal Bernard Law of Boston pulled out all the stops to promote this referendum, as well as an anti-abortion question that was also on the ballot. Pastoral statements from the state's bishops and sermons in parish churches attempted to get the message to the half of Massachusetts voters who are Catholic. Meanwhile, the measure's chief sponsor, State Senate President William Bulger of South Boston, raised the issue of anti-Catholicism, accusing opponents of Question 2 of bigotry.

Nonetheless, the voters turned down the proposal by a 70 percent to 30 percent margin. Every county and almost every voting precinct opposed it. Only in three Boston wards (including Bulger's South Boston district) and in the town of Webster did parochiaid triumph. Elsewhere, it was a disaster. Question 2 lost heavily in college towns like Amherst (86 percent against) and Cambridge (77 percent against) and upper-income Protestant Beacon Hill (80 percent against).

But parochiaid also failed in working-class Catholic towns like Gloucester (76 percent against), New Bedford (60 percent against), and Chelsea (63 percent against). In other such Catholic strongholds as Holyoke, Springfield, Lawrence, and Lowell, a majority of voters rejected the parochiaid lobby.

1986: South Dakota

The parochiaiders won their only victory in the past quarter century when voters approved a textbook loan proposal by a 54 percent majority. Sponsored by Republican Governor William Janklow, a conservative Lutheran, the proposal, Amendment C, was apparently considered a relatively harmless indirect form of aid in this predominantly Lutheran state. Public educators and civil libertarians estimated the proposal would cost the state about $2 million yearly.

1990: Oregon

Despite being outspent at least two to one, Oregon's defenders of church-state separation and public education won a solid 67 percent victory at the polls on November 6. At issue in the referendum was a proposed tuition tax credit of $2,500 per child for students who attend parochial and private schools or who are educated at home. The proposal would have cost taxpayers from $60 to $100 million per year.

The amount reported in the press just prior to election day showed $260,000 in expenditures for the scheme's front group, Oregonians for Educational Choice. However, out-of-state support for this costly and unconstitutional parochiaid scheme amounted to an amazing 93 percent of total funding. A $60,000 donation came from the Washington, D.C.-based Citizens for a Sound Economy (CSE), a group that supports "free-market economic policies and supply-side economics," according to its media relations director, Sedef Onder. CSE, founded in 1984, claims 250,000 members nationwide. Ms. Onder said the group had used Oregon as an "experiment" in grassroots advocacy.

Other supporters of the proposal included Vice-President J. Danforth Quayle, voucher advocate John Chubb of the Brookings Institution, conservative economist Milton Friedman, conservative guru William F. Buckley, Jr., and former Secretary of Education William Bennett. The far right advocates included Paul Weyrich's Free Congress Foundation, Phyllis Schlafly's Eagle Forum, and Beverly LaHaye's Concerned Women for America.

Supporters of church-state separation and public education raised $130,000, almost all of it from in-state. Oregon teachers organizations and the National Education Association spearheaded these efforts.

LESSONS OF THE REFERENDA

Advocates of tax aid or support for sectarian and other nonpublic schools often claim wide support for their point of view. Their claims, however, are usually based on poorly designed poll questions. While permitting families greater choice among public schools is at least a superficially popular idea, mixing together public school choice and tax support for nonpublic schools in a single poll question to be answered yes or no is sure to produce ambiguous if not meaningless results.

However, when the issue is placed concretely before a large group

TABLE 8

STATE REFERENDA ON PAROCHIAID, 1966–1990

YEAR	STATE	% AGAINST	% FOR
1966	Nebraska	57%	43%
1967	New York	72%	27%
1970	Nebraska	57%	43%
1970	Michigan	57%	43%
1972	Oregon	61%	39%
1972	Idaho	57%	43%
1972	Maryland	55%	45%
1974	Maryland	57%	43%
1975	Washington	60%	40%
1976	Alaska	54%	46%
1976	Missouri	60%	40%
1978	Michigan	74%	26%
1981	District of Columbia	89%	11%
1982	California	61%	39%
1982	Massachusetts	62%	38%
1986	Massachusetts	70%	30%
1986	South Dakota	46%	54%
1990	Oregon	67%	33%

of voters, with advocates and opponents of the proposed constitutional amendment or law slugging it out in the public arena and the media, then a meaningful test of public opinion is possible. As we have seen, electorates educated about the parochiaid issue in a rough-and-tumble election campaign almost invariably (94 percent of the time in the last quarter century) vote no on diverting public funds to nonpublic schools, even though the opponents are almost always outspent by a considerable margin.

Other valid tests of public opinion occurred in the 1970s when the Nixon and Ford administrations put considerable effort and money into trying to get individual school districts to experiment with federally funded voucher schemes. Despite all that effort, only one district in the nation, the Alum Rock district in San Jose, California, agreed to participate in a three-year experiment, and only after stipulating that no religious schools whatever be involved. The experiment was not considered a success. Efforts by the Ford administration to sell a federally funded voucher plan to communities in New Hampshire and Connecticut came to naught when local opinion polls, sponsored by the voucher promoters, consistently rejected the plans.

Promoting parochiaid, then, would seem to be the wrong horse for a politician to hitch a wagon to, although some politicians in some areas might gain from it. Parochiaid supporters are more likely than parochiaid opponents to be single-issue voters.

Unfortunately, the parochiaiders' horrendous losing streak is not widely known. For obscure reasons about which we can only speculate, the media have largely ignored this quarter-century of electoral defeats for parochiaid. They rarely rate a mention outside the states in which they occur, and generally receive far less coverage than referenda on far less significant matters.

The American people, it is safe to conclude, support public education and do not want to be taxed to aid or support nonpublic, mainly sectarian schools

NOTES

1. The full story of the New York referendum is told in Edd Doerr, *The Conspiracy That Failed* (Silver Spring, Md.: Americans United, 1968).

2. James E. Adams, "Warns of Catholic Backlash on Schools," *St. Louis Post-Dispatch,* August 8, 1976.

3. Allison Finn, "Wording Confused Some Voters," *Columbia Missourian,* August 6, 1976.

6

The Federal Battle

Parochiaid advocates in Congress began to propose aid schemes in the late 1940s. Congressmen from heavily Catholic states like Massachusetts introduced bills providing for construction grants and so-called "child benefit" assistance, but they were routinely defeated. In 1960, Senator Wayne Morse of Oregon, a liberal Democrat and a Protestant, surprised many people with his amendment proposing construction grants for church-related schools. It, too, was defeated, with most Protestants opposed and all Catholics—except for Massachusetts Senator John F. Kennedy—in favor.

The election of America's first Catholic president, John F. Kennedy, later that year led to a dramatic fight that electrified the nation and highlighted the important political dimension of this issue. If there was any one domestic issue about which Kennedy felt strongly, it was education. "He devoted more time . . . to this single topic than to any other domestic issue," his biographer, Ted Sorensen, observed.[1] Kennedy believed that the federal government had a legitimate need and an awesome historic responsibility to improve public education at every level and to make it possible for every deserving child to obtain as much education as possible. He tried for an omnibus bill for education; but when it was blocked by standpatters in Congress, he sought categorical grants for specific programs. He sought to extend the National Defense Education Act (NDEA) of 1958 and to aid universities in the Higher Education Facilities Act of 1963.

Kennedy also favored aid to teachers' salaries, classroom construction, expanded library facilities, new vocational-technical centers, federally approved or guaranteed scholarship loans for needy students, literacy programs, aid to retarded and handicapped children, school lunch and library programs, and educational television. The Office of Education called the Kennedy legislative proposals the most far-reaching in a century.

There was a fly in the ointment, however. Roman Catholic lobbyists, primarily in the National Catholic Welfare Conference (NCWC) —now the U.S. Catholic Conference—demanded that parochial schools be included in all federal programs. This had been a long-standing NCWC policy position and they saw no reason to alter it because a Catholic was now president. Southern conservatives and segregationists, who feared federal pressure for civil rights and equal educational opportunities for blacks, as well as Republican conservatives, who opposed all federal aid to education on ideological grounds, allied themselves with the NCWC. Even before Inauguration Day, Cardinal Francis Spellman of New York, the semi-official U.S. primate, blasted the Kennedy task force report on education as "unthinkable" for not including parochial schools. The president was outraged at Spellman's intransigence and told Sorensen, "He never said a word about any of Eisenhower's bills for public schools only, and he didn't go that far in 1949 either."[2]

Kennedy refused to budge. He presented his program in Congress and excluded sectarian schools "in accordance with the clear prohibition of the Constitution." The NCWC immediately called for the defeat of all federal aid to education unless loans to parochial schools were included. Kennedy tartly commented at a press conference a few days later: "The Catholic, Protestant, and Jewish clergy are entitled to their views, but they should not change their views merely because of the religion of the occupant of the White House."[3]

At the president's press conference on March 1, 1961, the question of federal aid to parochial schools was raised. Kennedy replied: "There isn't any room for debate on that subject. It is prohibited by the Constitution and the Supreme Court has made that very clear. Therefore, there would have been no possibility of our recommending it."

The Catholic bishops were not long in replying—one day later, to be specific. In a hurriedly convened special session they discussed the matter. There was considerable apprehension about forcing a showdown with the nation's first Catholic president so early in his administration. But in the end Cardinal Spellman's will prevailed and the bishops committed themselves to seeking the defeat of any aid to education measures which "discriminated" against their institutions. They said: "In the event that a federal aid program is enacted which excludes children in private schools, these children will be the victims of discriminatory legislation. . . . There will be no alternative but to oppose such discrimination."

As the battle mounted in intensity, Kennedy asked for a memorandum on the subject of constitutionality of federal aid to church schools. The "Memorandum on the First Amendment to the Constitution Upon Federal Aid to Education" was prepared and issued jointly by the Justice Department and the Department of Health, Education, and Welfare on March 28, 1961. (Paul Blanshard was a consultant and actually drafted much of the memorandum.) It said in part: "Federal grants to sectarian schools for general educational purposes would run squarely into the prohibitions of the First Amendment as interpreted in the *Everson, McCollum,* and *Zorach* cases. Grants of assistance in the construction of school facilities and for increasing teachers' salaries . . . are a clear case of what is proscribed by the Constitution. . . . Aid by way of grants to sectarian schools could only be justified by a reversal of the Supreme Court's interpretation of the establishment clause and a new interpretation which would regard it as merely prohibiting discrimination among religions."[4]

Kennedy was incensed when Spellman claimed that passage of the bill would mean the end of parochial schools in the United States. Spellman seemed to have forgotten that parochial schools were doing well in 1961, and were continuing to attract almost half of the Catholic school-age children without public support. For generations poor Catholic immigrants had provided for their own schools and had not sought public funds. Many Catholic laypeople, both liberal and conservative, opposed public aid.

The Kennedy bill passed the Senate, but the real battle was destined to be the House. The parochiaid lobby's auxiliary arm, Citizens for Educational Freedom (CEF), called for a nationwide campaign to block the Kennedy bill, threatening to defeat any member of Congress opposed to aiding church schools.

Cardinal Spellman pounded the pavements, contending that Kennedy's proposal "discriminates against Catholics who choose a God-centered education," was an effort "to use economic compulsion to force parents to relinquish their rights to have religion taught to their children," and constituted a deprivation of "freedom of religion." Most Protestant and Jewish leaders roundly denounced Spellman and urged acceptance of the Kennedy plan to aid the starved, underfunded public schools. Five national Jewish organizations issued a joint statement, saying, in part, "We deem the maintenance and furtherance of the Jewish religion to be the responsibility of the Jewish community, a responsibility which we have no desire to impose upon the American taxpayer."[5]

One needed a scorecard to tell the players in Congress. Senator Joseph Clark (D–Penn.), a Unitarian liberal Democrat and Kennedy supporter, announced that he would introduce the loan amendment that the bishops demanded. Senator Mike Mansfield (D–Mont.), majority leader of the Senate and a Catholic, sided with the president. Many Catholic congressmen felt torn loyalties in the Kennedy–Spellman clash. Representative John W. McCormack of Massachusetts, Democratic majority leader of the House, supported the bishops and pleaded for long-term low interest loans for construction of nonpublic schools.

Most Catholic journals supported the hierarchy, with the notable exception of *Commonweal*, the voice of progressive, enlightened Catholicism. Boston's Cardinal Richard Cushing, always the loyal friend, tried to use his influence to support the president's plan. Cushing had long opposed aid to parochial schools because of his fear of government entanglement and control. Cushing urged Catholics to recognize the strength of opposition to parochiaid and "neither [to] force such legislation through at the expense of national disunity nor use their political influence in Congress to block other legislation of benefit to education because they do not get their own way."[6]

Commonweal editorialized on July 7, 1961: "We think the administration's general aid to education bill should be passed." It blasted the two Catholic members of the Rules Committee, James Delaney and Thomas P. ("Tip") O'Neill, for keeping the bill bottled up in committee. Such an action was "arbitrary, undemocratic . . . circumvention of the legislative process. Not least among the regrettable aspects of the Delaney–O'Neill maneuver is that it may rekindle animosities." *Commonweal* also published a piece by Father George H. Dunne, who contended that "American Catholics should be happy that the President takes the position he does. . . . It is surely in the interest of the church in the United States that the first Catholic President prove beyond any shadow of doubt that his political judgments are not subject to dictation by the hierarchy."[7]

America magazine's erstwhile education specialist, Father Charles M. Whelan, while defending parochiaid as both constitutional and necessary for educational pluralism and religious liberty, also recognized "another Catholic position" that was "wholly consistent" with the hierarchy's. "It emphasizes that the church is essentially a religious society and must be willing to suffer temporal injustice rather than be identified simply as one more political pressure group." Whelan went on to say: "When a particular program threatens to distort the public image of the church, that program calls for special scrutiny. The Catholic appeal for federal aid to church schools, as widely interpreted in the nation today, does distort the public image of the church. We stand accused by men of good will of placing our special interests above the general welfare."[8]

Kennedy aide Ralph Dungan, HEW Secretary Abraham Ribicoff, and adviser Theodore Sorensen tried to convince the bishops and their staff that Kennedy's proposals were sound, constitutional, and in no way anti-Catholic. The administration, they contended, had no objections to purely peripheral school lunches, health services, or transportation services being extended to nonpublic school children. But to no avail. If parochial schools were excluded, the bishops said, no aid should go to public schools.

Major Protestant bodies joined the National Education Association and other groups in opposing any inclusion of parochial schools in federal aid programs. Dr. Gerald E. Knoff, an official with the National Council of Churches, testified on March 16, 1961, before the House Subcommittee on Education. His views epitomize the anti-parochiaid position.

Nothing is more clear than the likelihood that if substantial grants or loans to church-related elementary and secondary schools were made possible, many religious denominations would come to the conclusion that they too should step forward to the public treasury and claim what they would consider their share of federal funds.

If this should happen we believe that our American democracy would be impaired by the increasing fragmentation of education with its inevitable result of cultural segregation. Public schools would be undermined and a cultural schism would develop which would tend to impair our democracy.

The denominations of the National Council of Churches do not believe that such a development would be for the good of our beloved America, no matter what church or synagogue our people worship in and no matter what schools their children attend from Monday morning to Friday afternoon.[9]

The *Christian Century* expressed a view common to Protestants of all persuasions. "Charges that the omission of parochial schools from the administration's education bill is a discrimination against Roman Catholics is wholly without foundation. The Roman Catholic hierarchy in its condemnation of the Kennedy bill and in its warning that it will fight any bill which does not include aid to parochial schools is demanding not equality but preference and patronage. Such a claim cannot be granted within the provisions of the Constitution and under the plain restrictions of the First Amendment."[10]

The secular press, including the *New York Times*, the *Washington Post*, the *Washington Star*, and most liberal independent journals supported the Kennedy position. *U.S. News and World Report* and *Life*, which had supported Nixon in 1960, supported the Catholic hierarchy's position. A Gallup poll in late April found that 57 percent of voters wanted public funds confined to public schools, while 36 percent wanted both parochial and private schools included. Protestants were 63 to 29 percent for public school aid only, while Catholics were 66 to 28 percent in favor of parochiaid. On that issue the president's position was clearly the majority one. Once again Kennedy espoused a position not in favor with the majority of his co-religionists.

Late in July the die was cast. The House Rules Committee, by an eight to seven vote, killed the Kennedy bills and made it impossible for them to be considered again without invoking the rarely used discharge petition or suspension of rules. The key vote was cast by Representative James J. Delaney, a conservative Catholic Democrat from Queens, New York, who was regarded as the closest thing to a "professional" Catholic lobbyist in Congress. (He was immensely popular in his district and received Republican as well as Democratic votes.) Delaney was regarded as "Spellman's man" and was widely blamed or praised for the defeat of the entire Kennedy federal aid package. *Church & State* (September 1961) called the defeat an example of "clerical blackmail."

The complexity of the Rules Committee vote was lost on some. The committee was supposed to consider both Kennedy's omnibus bill for public schools and a bill that had just passed the House Education and Labor Committee, providing for $375 million in loans through NDEA for nonpublic schools. The loans would be given for the construction of classrooms and laboratory facilities for the teaching of mathematics, foreign languages, and science. The bill was opposed by the NEA and strict separationists. Representative Delaney, the apparent swing vote, insisted that all bills be rewritten into one measure, in effect making parochiaid part of a package deal. To get aid for public schools, members would have to vote to include parochials. When this move was defeated, Delaney said he wanted "to clear the air" and voted against all aid.

Given the interfaith tensions, it was understandable that Protestants would blame Delaney and, by extension, the Roman Catholic Church for the defeat. *Christian Century*, in an angry editorial, "Hierarchy Kills School Aid," said: "Federal aid to public education is dead. The hierarchy of the Roman Catholic Church cannot escape —indeed, is probably willing to accept—blame for the death blow to Kennedy's education proposals. . . . The hierarchy unabashedly put its special pleas ahead of the nation's needs and threatened to pull down the whole house if it could not have its way."[11] It charged that the hierarchy had shown "no catholicity of charity, justice, or concern" but rather had engaged in "short-sighted, indulged self-interest." In an accompanying editorial, however, the *Century* hailed the favorable votes of the other two Catholic congressmen ("Tip" O'Neill of Massachusetts and Ray Madden of Indiana), saying that they "are to be commended for rising above sectarian interests in their concern for the nation's problems." Most Protestant and secular journals agreed with the *Century*'s assessment. The Georgia Baptist weekly, *The Christian Index*, commented: "We were wrong about President Kennedy, but we were not wrong about the Roman Catholic Church. It is superb in the game of power politics. It demands instead of asking. It doesn't threaten reprisals, it guarantees them."[12]

A battle royal between Oregon's choleric Senator Wayne Morse and Cardinal Francis Spellman added to the August heat. Morse blasted the bishops in an address to the American Federation of Teachers:

I have no intention of compromising the principles of federal aid to education with any pressure group, or private school group in America, who seek to take federal aid to education legislation into the political trading mart. . . . A third category of opponents of federal aid . . . include highly influential churchmen such as Cardinal Spellman [who] look upon the public schools as competitors. They feel that pressures for improvement in teachers' salaries and reduction in pupil-teacher load in the public schools will result in a draining away of their own lay teachers. . . .

I appreciate the magnitude of the problem with which they are faced, but I say in all sincerity that the adamant opposition of the higher Catholic clergy to an improvement to our public educational system except upon their own terms will lead to most unfortunate results. If they succeed temporarily in blocking the legitimate aims of a majority of our people through pressure tactics, they are sowing a wind of discord which will result in a whirlwind of resentment when the people of the country learn the facts. . . .

I say again to the Catholic bishops, do not insist adamantly in this matter upon an all-or-nothing-at-all policy, for if you do, the latent religious quarrels of past history will be brought to life again, and the fabric of our civil society will be stretched once more to the breaking point.[13]

Cardinal Spellman retorted: "It is our conviction that the administration's proposal, put into legislative form by Senator Morse, is actually if not intentionally discriminatory, unwittingly anti-Catholic, and indirectly subversive of all private education."[14] Morse, however, had the last word in a Senate address: "The Cardinal cannot repeal the First Amendment by seeming to ignore it."

At their November 1961 annual meeting, the bishops reiterated their all-or-nothing position, and blasted the "discrimination" that Catholics suffer on the education question. The *New York Times* (November 18, 1961) called the bishops' statement "wholly misleading" and the *Washington Post* said that "public schools are open without the slightest discrimination to children of every creed."

The Apostolic Delegate, Archbishop Egidio Vagnozzi, rather unwisely waded into the stream of controversy in a November 14 address in Philadelphia. He told a conference of twelve hundred Catholic laymen to support the bishops against the president because "the bishops know what they are doing."

President Kennedy became a hero in the eyes of many heretofore critical Protestants. In May 1961, the Southern Baptist Convention passed a resolution commending Kennedy "for his insistence that the Constitution of the United States be followed in the matter of not giving federal aid to church schools."[15] Dr. W. A. Criswell of Dallas called upon Baptists "to stand behind President Kennedy and the Constitution."[16]

C. Stanley Lowell, associate director of Protestants and Other Americans United for Separation of Church and State, told the press that "we are extremely well pleased with President Kennedy" whose "strong stand . . . will reassure and inspire all who believe in the separation of church and state."[17] *Christianity Today* (February 16, 1961), *Christian Herald* (May 1961), and several Lutheran, Baptist, Methodist, and United Church of Christ journals hailed Kennedy's courage and tenacity in the face of strong ecclesiastical pressure. When his aid bill was again brought before Congress in 1962, it was again rejected by the same coalition. Protestant and Catholic responses were roughly the same.

President Kennedy felt that Catholics were being unfairly singled out for blame. After all, two of the three Catholic Democrats on the Rules Committee voted for his public education bill, while all Protestant Republicans opposed it. The bill's House sponsor was a Catholic. In one test vote, only six of 166 Republicans voted for it, and virtually all Southern segregationists voted against it. "That's who really killed the bill," Kennedy told Sorensen, "just as they've killed it for fifty years, not the Catholics."[18]

Kennedy was livid, however, about Cardinal Spellman's role, regarding it as proof that Spellman was a partisan Republican. After all, had not Spellman met President Eisenhower at the Newark airport and ridden with him in a limousine past cheering New York crowds on the day of the first Nixon–Kennedy debates? And had not Spellman and four of the American cardinals, in addition to nine archbishops and fifty-six bishops, sat on the dais during Eisenhower's address to the Golden Jubilee dinner of the National Conference of Catholic Charities? Eisenhower was, after all, campaigning for his heir apparent, Richard Nixon. This, plus the pro-Nixon enthusiasm at the Alfred E. Smith Memorial Dinner on October 19, 1960, convinced the Kennedy entourage that most of the American hierarchy and the Vatican itself preferred Nixon's election.

Cardinal Richard Cushing reminisced about those days in a 1964 interview.

Some of the hierarchy of the church, I presume, were not in favor of John F. Kennedy being elected President. Some of them had very strange ideas about the influence the millions of Catholics in the United States might exert on a man who would be the first President of the United States who was a Catholic. . . . On the matters of federal aid to Catholic education and related subjects, I think his attitude was correct. Some of the hierarchy, like myself, never enthused about such aid, for we presumed it would include some form of federal control. Furthermore, there were serious doubts about the constitutionality of such aid. . . . The members of the Catholic hierarchy who opposed the election of a Catholic President did so because they wished to be perfectly free in expressing opinions on public affairs and legislation that directly or indirectly referred to the freedom of religion.[19]

In other words, what Cushing seemed to be saying was that if certain members of the hierarchy could not control Kennedy, they would have preferred a more malleable Protestant, like Nixon.

Fletcher Knebel wrote at the height of the debate: "Whatever the final outcome of the school-aid fight in America—and it may go on for years—history will note that the country's first Catholic President fought side by side with Protestant leaders against the clergy of his own church."[20]

The tragic assassination of President Kennedy and the landslide reelection of his successor Lyndon Johnson changed the federal parochiaid picture in many ways. For one thing the Republicans, whose basic conservatism and localism tended to oppose federal aid for all schools, were routed in the Johnson sweep. They lost forty congressional seats and were reduced to their worst House showing since 1936. There remained some pro-parochiaid Catholics and segregationist Southern Democrats who opposed all federal aid, *but there was now a liberal majority committed to a comprehensive expansion of federal aid to public education.* Leo Pfeffer and C. Stanley Lowell, two authorities on church-state separation, were convinced that no capitulation to parochial school interests was politically necessary in 1965. But no one could have foreseen the subsequent intensity of the parochiaid campaign, the desire of President Johnson to please everyone, and the crucial support given to the politics of parochiaid by once-committed opponents in the Protestant and public education establishments. And it was President Lyndon Johnson himself who engineered the great reversal, even after specifically promising Texas

Baptist newspaper editor E. S. James in an October 1964 interview that he would not do so.

Stan Lowell, who was in the thick of the struggle over the proposed Elementary and Secondary Education Act of 1965 (ESEA), believes that Johnson's personality and long-term political strategy were instrumental in shaping the legislation. Lowell wrote:

> During the campaign of 1964, and even as Congress convened, Johnson never dealt directly with the issue of government aid to sectarian schools as Kennedy had done. He never discussed the matter openly and frankly, but talked vaguely of aiding all children. He promised to avoid the old church-state hang-up without ever indicating how he would do it. He never dealt in specifics with this question, offering, instead, just enough vague generality to give some comfort to everybody. Kennedy had been completely candid; Johnson was considerably less than candid. When Johnson finally came forward with his aid to education proposals, they offered major concessions to the Catholic Church. In doing so, they struck a heavy blow at separation of church and state. Yet even as the bill was introduced, it was accompanied by a continuing campaign of deception which sought to conceal its real nature from the American people.[21]

Roman Catholic educational lobbyists were astute and bold, and the support of House Speaker John McCormack was important. The ESEA was designed to help the educationally disadvantaged at every level and in every kind of school situation. It was historic and comprehensive in scope. But the inclusion of parochial schools as participants and recipients in the funding threatened the bill's success. Lowell credits Monsignor Frederick G. Hochwalt of the U.S. Catholic Conference for "one of the most intensive and astute legislative efforts ever seen in Congress."[22] "The church school compromise which eventually emerged," said Lowell, "was in substantial detail devised by Hochwalt and approved by him."[23]

The Johnson administration went to work on the Protestants, attempting to break down their traditional enmity to parochiaid. Brooks Hays, a former Arkansas congressman and "religious troubleshooter" for the president, and fellow Baptist staffer, Bill Moyers, convinced the Baptist Joint Committee on Public Affairs to drop its opposition, claiming the bill only aided children and not the religious institution. The Baptist Joint Committee director, C. Emanuel Carlson,

joined the consensus and engineered a Moyers appearance before
the annual meeting of the Southern Baptist Convention. Carlson
claimed that "most of the church-state issues in President Johnson's
education bill have been eliminated."[24]

The powerful National Council of Churches soon fell in line.
Its religious liberty executive, Dean M. Kelley, announced that the
"main Protestant bodies of the nation have found a common ground
with Roman Catholics on which they can accept the President's proposal for federal aid to educationally deprived children."[25]

Other prominent Protestant voices were added to the chorus of
approval, including Arthur S. Flemming of the National Council and
H. B. Sissel of the Presbyterians.

Still, there were nagging doubts about the constitutionality and
propriety of the landmark proposal. The old-line separationist groups,
including the American Civil Liberties Union, Americans United, the
American Jewish Congress, the Unitarian-Universalists, and the conservative National Association of Evangelicals, mounted an opposition
campaign. Their congressional leader, North Carolina Senator Sam
Ervin, tried to eliminate parochial schools by amendment and then
demanded a constitutional test. All of Ervin's valiant efforts failed
in floor votes.

As the legislation was being fine-tuned before final passage,
Representative Frank Thompson of New York told his fellow House
members how the bill would work:

> Services and arrangements provided for nonpublic school students in
> nonpublic schools must be special as distinguished from general edu-
> cational assistance. The decision about the best arrangement for pro-
> viding special educational assistance under Title I is left to the public
> education agency of the school district, under the Constitution and
> laws of the State. Thus, public school boards could make available
> the services of such special personnel as guidance counselors, speech
> therapists, remedial reading specialists, school social workers who would
> reach the nonpublic school children in the public schools, or through
> public services in the nonpublic buildings, or through mobile services,
> or through ETV [educational television], or through community cen-
> ters, etc.[26]

The legislation had three sections. "Title I provides 'special educational services and arrangements (such as dual enrollment), educational radio and television, and mobile educational services and equipment.' Title II provides for 'library resources, textbooks, and other instructional materials' for students in private schools. Title III provides that supplementary activities and services provided under the program 'are to be made available to students in private schools.' "[27]

The ESEA became law, but the church-state controversy did not end. Though "payments for religious worship or instruction" were banned in the legislation, church schools reaped a bonanza.

Stanley Lowell wrote angrily: "For amid the studied ambiguities of ESEA, grants were unquestionably flowing into church schools in a manner they had not contemplated. . . . A study of ESEA in the schools of New York City disclosed that sectarian interests in that area preempted the programs and operated them in a manner which showed gross favoritism to the children attending sectarian schools and discrimination against those attending public schools."[28]

Educational researcher George LaNoue, writing in the *Rutgers Law Review* (Winter 1968), found an almost total disregard for the church-state safeguards and restrictions in the administration of ESEA aid to church schools in sixty New Jersey school districts. Within a few years, criticism was mounting from around the country. The NAACP Legal Defense and Education Fund claimed that $1.4 million in Title I funds were being used to purchase Temple Baptist Church in Detroit under the pretext of placing a Title I projects administrative office there. Title II and III funds were disbursed to church schools with little or no monitoring. Writing in 1972, Stanley Lowell charged, "After six years of ESEA it is clear that the Federal Government is steadily channeling funds into church schools."[29]

Church-state separationists now began their counterattack. After successfully suing to prove that taxpayers had standing to challenge this kind of expenditure in *Flast* v. *Cohen*, the National Coalition for Public Education and Religious Liberty (PEARL) brought suit in 1976 against the Federal Department of Education and the New York City Board of Education (*PEARL* v. *Hufstedler and Anker*). For procedural and other reasons, a parallel case, *Felton* v. *Secretary, U. S. Department of Education*, was instituted.[30]

The district court upheld the Title I program in New York, ruling that the evidence produced at the trial failed to prove that advancement of religion was the purpose or primary effect of the program and that there was excessive government entanglement with religion.[31] In the *Felton* case, an appeals court ruled that the district court was wrong in the *PEARL* case, and that the U.S. Supreme Court ruling in *Meek* v. *Pittenger* should have been followed.

Leo Pfeffer describes the ruling:

> Specifically, it ruled that tax-raised funds could be used to accord remedial instruction or related counseling services to students in religious schools only if the instruction and services were accorded by publicly employed teachers and took place off the premises of the religious schools. Whatever the forms of state aid to religious elementary and secondary schools, the Court said, they must not create a risk sufficiently significant to require policing to assure that public school personnel will not act, even unwittingly, to foster religion. The Court stated in its opinion that a "fair" case could be made that the government's financing constituted a direct and substantial advancement of religious activity, as was the case in the *Meek* decision. It preferred, however, to rest its decision on the entanglement prohibition in the Establishment Clause [of the First Amendment].[32]

The U.S. Supreme Court had the last word in 1985. The basic question was whether Title I services to parochial school students could be provided on the premises of parochial schools. The Appeals Court had concluded: "The picture that emerges is of a system in which religious considerations play a key role in the selection of students and teachers, and which has as its substantial purpose the inculcation of religious values."[33] The five to four ruling of the High Court, written by Justice William J. Brennan, concluded in a strongly worded opinion: "Despite the well-intentioned efforts taken by the City of New York, the program remains constitutionally flawed owing to the nature of the aid, to the institution receiving the aid, and to the constitutional principles that they implicate—that neither the State nor Federal Government shall promote or hinder a particular faith or faith generally through the advancement of benefits or through the excessive entanglement of church and state in the administration of those benefits."[34]

Since the early 1970s there has been a continuing campaign on the federal level to enact a voucher scheme to finance nonpublic education under the guise of "choice." Under such a plan, parochial and private schools would be 100 percent tax-supported by means of government vouchers given to the parents of all school children. The vouchers, equivalent in value to the average amount normally spent per student per year in public schools, would be used by parents to pay tuition to the public, parochial, or private school of their choice provided the preferred school had room for and would accept their children.

The voucher plan was the brainchild of the Reverend Virgil Blum, a Jesuit political scientist at Marquette University and mentor of the predominantly Roman Catholic parochiaid lobby group, Citizens for Educational Freedom, founded in the late 1950s. Also advocating variations of the voucher plan were conservative economist Milton Friedman and liberal economist Christopher Jencks. Jencks became the Nixon administration's chief voucher theoretician, under planning grants from the Office of Economic Opportunity (OEO). (In 1969–1970 alone $521,143 was allotted for voucher experiments.) Under the OEO and later the National Institute of Education (NIE), federal grants for voucher plan feasibility studies were provided to a number of public school districts around the country. Every school board that ever considered the plan rejected it, with the exception of the Alum Rock District in San Jose, California, which accepted federal support for a voucher demonstration mainly as a way of getting badly needed additional funds and which confined the demonstration exclusively to public schools.

In January 1976, the East Hartford, Connecticut, school board voted the plan down after two opinion polls showed that the people of the heavily Catholic city opposed it by a 70 percent to 30 percent margin. The NIE had squandered $387,000 in public funds to persuade the people of East Hartford to accept the plan. In March of the same year the voters in the New Hampshire towns of Allentown, Candia, Deerfield, Hollis, Hooksett, and Salem voted strongly to spurn the plan before it could even be tried out. This occurred even though the NIE had spent $360,000 in public funds to design the plan and sell it to the people of the six towns, and although Governor Meldrim Thompson and State Board of Education Chairman William Bittenbender had supported the plan strongly.

Sporadic efforts have continued, particularly by the libertarian right wing, but Congress has never given the proposal significant support. However, there was a brief flurry of voucher activity during

Ronald Reagan's second term. In December 1985, Senator Orrin Hatch (R–Utah) and Representative Pat Swindall (R–Ga.) introduced a so-called "Equity and Choice Act" (S.1876 and H.R.3821). With the support of President Reagan and Secretary of Education William Bennett, the proposal was designed to give families of remedial students a $600 per year voucher for every child which could be cashed at any school. The primary beneficiaries were parochial and private schools. Critics charged that the proposal would surely be held unconstitutional under the *Nyquist* and other rulings.

In *Nyquist*, for example, the Supreme Court held: "By reimbursing parents for a portion of their tuition bill, the State seeks to relieve their financial burdens sufficiently to assure that they continue to have the option to send their children to religion-oriented schools. . . . [T]he effect of the aid is unmistakably to provide desired financial support for nonpublic, sectarian institutions."

Furthermore, the justices argued, "If the grants are offered as an incentive to parents to send their children to sectarian schools by making unrestricted cash payments to them, the Establishment Clause is violated. . . . Whether the grant is labeled a reimbursement, a reward, or a subsidy, its substantive impact is still the same."[35]

Few Americans liked the plan. Syndicated columnist Carl Rowan said it was "fantasy-land thinking" to suppose that a voucher plan would really benefit disadvantaged minority students. Only private schools would reap the benefits. The *Atlanta Constitution* called it "a sorry sham, a con on the poor," while the *Fort Worth Star Telegram* opined: "It does not take a Socrates to figure out that the voucher proposal would mainly benefit the parochial schools and the parents who, for religious reasons, would like some help in paying the bills for a religious-oriented education for their children. Neither does it take a genius to figure out that the vouchers would spell doom for many public schools."[36]

Tax credits posed a more formidable challenge. On September 26, 1977, Senators Robert Packwood (R–Or.), Daniel P. Moynihan (D–N.Y.), and 41 of their colleagues introduced their Tuition Tax Credit Act of 1977, S.2142, in the Senate. A companion bill, H.R. 9332, was then introduced in the House of Representatives by Representatives Bill Frenzel (R–Minn.), Tom Railsback (R–Ill.), and James A. Burke (D–Mass.).

The Packwood–Moynihan plan would have pumped more than

$3 billion in federal funds annually into parochial and private schools and into church-related and other private colleges. To sweeten the plan and give it a greater chance of passage, the bill also provided more than $2.5 billion annually to public colleges and a wide assortment of vocational schools.

Under the Packwood–Moynihan plan, the federal aid would be delivered through tuition reimbursements of 50 percent of tuition up to a maximum benefit of $500 per student. The tuition reimbursements would be provided through a combination of federal income tax credits and outright grants (misleadingly labelled "tax refunds") for persons whose tuition reimbursement tax credits exceed their tax liability.

That the Packwood–Moynihan bill was intended to alter the First Amendment's ban on tax aid for parochial schools is evident when the bill's architects are examined. They included Monsignor Edward Spiers, executive director of Citizens for Educational Freedom; the Reverend Donald Shea, the Catholic priest and director of the Republican National Committee's Ethnic/Catholic division; the Reverend Virgil Blum, S.J., long-time mentor and principal spokesman for parochiaid; the Reverend James Burtchaell, former provost of Notre Dame University; and the Reverend Charles Whelan, S.J., a church-state expert on the Fordham Law School faculty and one-time adviser to former President Nixon's parochiaid-minded Commission on School Finance. Spiers, Blum, and Whelan were long-time advocates of tax support for parochial schools. Also called in as advisers were Dr. Robert Lamborn of the Council on American Private Education and Al Sinske, a Missouri Synod Lutheran parochiaid promoter.

Nor was there any great mystery behind the bill's large number of 43 Senate sponsors, of whom the majority (25) were Republicans. The Republican Party, having been reduced to minority party status vis-à-vis the Democrats, has put a large stack of chips on the "Catholic strategy" developed nearly a decade ago by former President Nixon and campaign manager John Mitchell, as chronicled by conservative columnist Kevin Phillips. The idea is to woo ethnic blue-collar urban Catholic voters away from the Democrats by promising tax aid for parochial schools as part of a conservative social strategy.

This is evidently why Senator Packwood, a Unitarian from a state with few parochial schools and relatively few Catholic voters, was selected to be the leading sponsor of the tuition reimbursement bill. Senator Moynihan, a Catholic Democrat who had been pushing for parochiaid since 1961, made an ideal co-sponsor for the bill from the point of view of the bill's party and clerical designers.

The Packwood–Moynihan bill represented a confluence of Catholic hierarchy and Republican Party leadership interests. This was reflected in the makeup of the 43 sponsors of S.21241: 25 Republicans and 18 Democrats in a Democratic dominated Senate; 35 Protestants, six Catholics and two Jews; 24 Westerners, ten Easterners, and nine from Southern and border states. (The bill attracted 60 percent of the Senate's Republicans, but only 30 percent of its Democrats; the most likely supporter of the bill tended to be a moderate Republican from the West.) Of the three House sponsors, Frenzel was a religiously unaffiliated Minnesota Republican; Railsback, an Illinois Republican, and member of the United Church of Christ, while James Burke was a Roman Catholic Massachusetts Democrat.

This religio-political confluence threatened to politicize religion and inject religion into politics, a development which the Supreme Court has said the First Amendment was adopted in part to prevent. The Republican National Committee's Reverend Shea was reportedly assigned the task, more than a year before the 1978 Congressional elections, of traveling around the country to translate this religio-political tax credit ploy into votes in November 1978.

Hearings on the Packwood–Moynihan tuition reimbursement bill began in the Senate Finance Committee in early January 1978. Often acrimonious hearings were held in Congress for eight days during the first two months of 1978—three days of hearings in the Senate in January and five days in the House in February. Out of more than 120 witnesses at the hearings, a majority testified in favor of the Packwood–Moynihan bill. The parochiaiders parading before the two Congressional committees appeared to be well coordinated, prepared, and choreographed.

Senator Moynihan dominated the Senate hearings with demagogic monologues, frequently denouncing opposition to parochiaid as a residue of "nineteenth-century nativist bigotry." He bitterly attacked the Carter administration's opposition to the bill and accused President Carter of reneging on a campaign promise to aid parochial schools. The truth that Moynihan chose to ignore, however, is that Carter expressed interest during his 1976 campaign only in finding "constitutional" ways of aiding parents of parochial school students.

The Carter administration viewed the tuition reimbursement scheme as unconstitutional and excessively expensive.*

Constitutional lawyer Leo Pfeffer, representing two dozen religious, educational, civil liberties, and civic groups in the National Coalition for Public Education and Religious Liberty, traced the U.S. Supreme Court rulings on parochiaid and concluded that the Packwood–Moynihan bill was clearly unconstitutional as applied to parochial schools. Florence Flast, of the New York Committee for Public Education and Religious Liberty (PEARL), warned that racial imbalance would result from tax-supported private schools. The Ohio Free Schools Association's Gaston D. Cogdell warned, "The parochial schools themselves will become less and less responsive to private and church influence and will come under increasing government control."[37]

HEW Secretary Joseph Califano warned that President Carter would veto any tuition tax credit legislation sent to his desk. On March 17, the Justice Department issued a memorandum holding that the tax credit scheme would be held unconstitutional by the Supreme Court. At a meeting of the American Society of Newspaper Editors on April 11, President Carter said, "My present intention would be to veto any bill that was costly and unconstitutional. I don't favor tuition tax credits under any circumstances. . . ."[38] Vice-President Walter Mondale told an anti-parochiaid group meeting at the White House on April 11 that the tax credit plan would lead to "further erosion and weakening of the public schools."[39] NEA President John Ryor, at a press conference the day before, was angered by charges that opponents of tax credits were anti-Catholic. "I am a Catholic. The legislators who oppose this bill are not anti-Catholic," he reiterated.[40]

Also testifying against the bill at the hearings were representatives of the U.S. Departments of Treasury and Health, Education, and Welfare; the Baptist Joint Committee on Public Affairs; the New York Coalition for Public Education and Religious Liberty; the National Council of Jewish Women; the National School Boards Association; the National Education Association; the American Federation of Teachers; the National Congress of Parents and Teachers; the Wis-

---

*The Legal Division of the Library of Congress issued a memorandum on August 12, 1977, pointing out that the tax credit and grant plan for aiding parochial schools was unconstitutional under the Supreme Court's 1973 *Nyquist* ruling.

consin Education Association; Preserve Our Public Schools of Wisconsin; the National Association of (Catholic) Laity; the Ohio Free Schools Association; and the Educational Policy Research Center for Higher Education.

Although Roman Catholic Church officials provided most of the pressure behind the Packwood–Moynihan bill, Catholics testifying against the bill included HEW Secretary Joseph Califano, Representative Charles W. Whelan, Jr. (R–Oh.), Dr. Joseph Skehan, president of the National Association of (Catholic) Laity, John Ryor, president of the National Education Association, and Paul de Vair, president of the Wisconsin Education Association.

The parochiaiders tried to distinguish the Packwood–Moynihan parochiaid plan from the almost identical state plans ruled unconstitutional by the Supreme Court. Parochiaid advocates testifying in favor of the bill included spokesmen for Citizens for Educational Freedom, the Federation of Catholic Teachers, the National Association of Catholic School Teachers, Agudath Israel of America (an Orthodox Jewish group), the Council for American Private Education, the National Association of Independent Schools, the Lutheran Church-Missouri Synod Board of Parish Education, the New York State Federation of Catholic School Parents, the Catholic Archdiocese of Philadelphia, Christian School Action, the Maryland Federation of Catholic Laity, the National Catholic Educational Association, and the Western Association of Christian Schools.

In April the House Ways and Means Committee voted 20 to 16 to delete parochial schools from the tax credit bill. (It had already passed the Senate Finance Committee.) A major confrontation was now inescapable.

On June 1 the full House approved the tax credit plan for parochial schools by 209 to 194, and then approved the entire bill by 237 to 158. The key vote on parochiaid was the former one. It was the first major parochiaid victory at the federal level in U.S. history.

The 209 to 194 vote revealed sharp religious, political, and regional differences. Roman Catholics voted three to one for tax credits, though Catholic Democrats favored it less strongly than Catholic Republicans. Jewish Democrats opposed it two to one though Jewish Republicans all voted for it. Protestant Democrats voted against the measure by nearly three to one while Protestant Republicans voted for it by about five to two. Among the Protestants, Baptists, Methodists, Unitarians, and United Church of Christ members were most opposed. Presbyterians and Lutherans tended to favor tax credits while the middle-road Episcopalians were evenly divided.

Representatives from states with above-average concentrations of parochial schools and powerful parochiaid lobbies voted for tax credits 71 percent to 29 percent. The Ohio and Pennsylvania delegations were—not surprisingly—overwhelmingly in favor of tuition tax credits. Even in those nine states where voters opposed parochiaid in referenda from 1966 to 76, a solid 60 percent of their representatives nodded assent. (The breakdown on this crucial vote is shown in Table 9.)

The battle now moved to the Senate, where defenders of church-state separation and religious liberty waged their last—and ultimately successful—venture. Leaders of the opposition included South Carolina's Ernest Hollings, who said House passage represented "a direct and ominous attack on the public school system."[41] Senator Edward Kennedy also blasted the proposal. On the Senate floor they were joined by Arkansas Democrat Kaneaster Hodges, a United Methodist minister.

On August 15th, the U.S. Senate dealt the fatal blow to decades of scheming and planning. By a 56 to 41 margin the Senators rejected the plan. In the upper chamber there was much greater Catholic opposition. Only 57 percent of Catholics voted yes. Among the opponents were Maine's Ed Muskie and Missouri's Tom Eagleton. Democrats were opposed by 68 percent but Republicans favored it by 59 percent. There was considerably more Republican opposition in the Senate than in the House. In the Senate 60 percent of Jews and 59 percent of Protestants were opposed, with Baptists, Methodists, and Presbyterians leading the opposition.

As an afterglow to this event, eight days later the Senate voted down a parochiaid plan for "auxiliary services," viz., transportation and loans to parochial schools. This little-noticed scheme introduced by Rhode Island's Claiborne Pell was defeated in a 60–30 vote. A last-ditch effort to restore some tax credits to the tax reform bill on October 14, 1978, with the 95th Congress winding down, also came to nothing. Conference committees rejected any and all attempts by parochiaiders to circumvent the August defeat in the Senate.

The Senate's leading parochiaider, Daniel Moynihan, admitted defeat, although not graciously. In a letter to the Catholic bishops, he wrote, "The institutions associated with social progress in American culture at this time are overwhelmingly against us on this issue."[42]

TABLE 9

HOUSE VOTE ON TUITION TAX CREDITS

JUNE 1, 1978

By Religion	Total		Democrats		Republicans	
	% For	% Against	% For	% Against	% For	% Against
Catholic	74.8	25.2	70.6	29.4	90.0	9.1
Protestant	43.2	56.8	25.5	74.5	70.8	29.2
Jewish	45.5	54.5	33.3	66.7	100.0	0.0
Subgroups						
Baptist	28.9	71.1	22.6	77.4	57.1	42.9
Episcopalian	50.0	50.0	29.2	70.8	77.8	22.2
Lutheran	58.3	41.7	33.3	66.7	66.7	33.3
Methodist	35.1	64.9	25.0	75.0	52.4	47.6
Presbyterian	54.2	45.8	30.8	69.2	81.8	18.2
Unitarian Universalist	14.3	85.7	0.0	100.0	100.0	0.0
United Church of Christ	33.3	66.7	10.0	90.0	80.0	20.0

	% For	% Against
All Democrats	40.4	59.6
All Republicans	75.2	24.8
Total	51.9	48.1

This remains largely true today. Even after more than a decade of Republican presidencies, and a Republican-dominated Senate for six years, no great movement for parochiaid at the federal level has emerged. The thrust remains at the state level, where, lamentably, it has gained momentum.

NOTES

1. Theodore Sorensen, *Kennedy* (New York: Harper & Row, 1965), p. 358.

2. Ibid., p. 360.

3. *Washington Post*, March 16, 1961.

4. C. Stanley Lowell, *The Great Church-State Fraud* (Washington, D.C.; New York: Robert B. Luce, 1973), pp. 25–26.

5. "The Public Schools," *Church & State* 14 (March 1961): 2.

6. Sorensen, *Kennedy*, p. 363.

7. *Commonweal*, June 2, 1961, pp. 247–50.

8. Rev. Charles M. Whelan, "School Question: Stage Two," *America*, April 1, 1961, pp. 17–19.

9. "National Council Representative Opposes Church School Loans,'" *Church & State* 14 (May 1961): 1.

10. "Catholics Demand Patronage," *Christian Century*, March 22, 1961, pp. 381–82.

11. "Hierarchy Kills School Aid," *Christian Century*, August 2, 1961, p. 924.

12. "Church Blocks Federal Funds," *Christian Index*, June 29, 1961, p. 6.

13. "Morse vs. Spellman," *Church & State* 14 (October 1961): 3, 5.

14. Ibid.

15. *Annual* of the Southern Baptist Convention, 1961, p. 81.

16. Sorensen, *Kennedy*, p. 363.

17. Ibid.

18. Ibid., p. 362.

19. Oral interview with Cardinal Cushing, in the archives of the John F. Kennedy Library.

20. Fletcher Knebel, "The Bishops vs. Kennedy," *Look*, May 9, 1961.

21. Lowell, *The Great Church-State Fraud*, p. 29.

22. Ibid., p. 29.

23. Ibid., p. 31.

24. Ibid., p. 31.

25. Ibid., p. 32.

26. *Congressional Record*, 1965, p. 5572.

27. Ibid.

28. Lowell, *The Great Church-State Fraud*, pp. 37, 39.

29. Ibid., p. 44.

30. For an illuminating commentary on these developments, see Leo Pfeffer, *Religion, State and the Burger Court* (Buffalo, N.Y.: Prometheus Books, 1984), pp. 45–53.

31. 449 US 808 [1980], 489 F.Supp. 1248.

32. Pfeffer, *Religion, State, and the Burger Court*, p. 51.

33. As quoted in *Aguilar* v. *Felton* 105 S Ct 33232.

34. Ibid.

35. 413 US 756 (1973).

36. "A Choice Reaction," *Church & State* 39 (January 1986): 4–6; "Parochiaid Crusade," *Church & State* 38 (December 1985): 4–6.

37. "The Parochiaid Blitz in Congress," *Church & State* 31 (March 1978): 8.

38. "Congress Faces Parochiaid Showdown," *Church & State* 31 (May 1978): 2.

39. Ibid., p. 7.

40. Ibid.

41. "Tax Credit Parochiaid," *Church & State* 31 (July–August 1978): 6.

42. "Tax Credits Defeated," *Church & State* 31 (November 1978): 6.

7

Parochiaid and the Courts

HISTORY

Before reviewing the relevant court rulings on parochiaid, it might be appropriate to touch briefly upon some of the highlights of the history of the controversy. New York State was the locus of the earliest American battles over tax aid for church schools. Requests for aid for Baptist schools led to action by the New York City Common Council in 1825 to bar such aid. Requests for aid for Catholic schools in the early 1840s led to a prolonged political donnybrook which resulted in passage of state legislation in 1844 barring aid to all schools "in which the religious sectarian doctrine or tenet of any particular Christian or other religious sect shall be taught, inculcated, or practiced." The battle was renewed in the 1890s and led to the inclusion of a strong provision, Article XI, Section 3, in the state constitution barring all aid to religious schools.[1]

Lowell, Massachusetts, maintained two Catholic schools as public schools until 1855, when the state constitution was amended to block tax aid to church schools.[2] A similar plan for providing public aid to parochial schools begun in the late nineteenth century was the Faribault Plan, named for the Minnesota town in which it originated. The plan, called the "captive school" plan by its opponents, involved the incorporation of parochial schools into public school systems. The plan led to bitter controversies in Ohio and other states as well as to state supreme court rulings against the plan in Missouri in

111

1942 and in New Mexico in 1951.[3] The practice continues in a few communities around the country, and attempts to revive it were made in Detroit and Milwaukee in 1990 and 1991.

Court decisions on laws providing tax aid to or for parochial education involve both federal and state constitutions and both federal and state courts. Before 1968, when the Supreme Court ruled that taxpayers have standing to sue in federal courts to challenge government expenditures alleged to violate the First Amendments's Establishment Clause,[4] suits attacking parochial aid measures had to be brought in state courts. Since 1968 the federal courts have been frequently chosen for attacks on state parochiaid plans because they have generally provided faster relief and earlier access to the Supreme Court. What has emerged is what appears from a distance to be a less than totally consistent pattern of Supreme Court and state court decisions on parochiaid, with the federal courts sometimes taking the harder line against such aid, while at other times the state courts have been more strongly opposed to parochiaid. What becomes obvious from the cases is that no judicial *deus ex machina* is likely to drop onto the stage and settle the parochiaid controversy simply and clearly for all times, especially after the appointments made by President Reagan to the Supreme Court.

Before the major parochiaid rulings of the Supreme Court beginning in 1971, the parochiaid controversy swirled around indirect aids, such as transportation and textbook loans.

The growing use of busing to enable public schools in rural and suburban areas to gather students from distances too great to walk led to demands for similar service for parochial schools. Before the Supreme Court considered this issue in *Everson* v. *Board of Education* in 1947,[5] a number of parochial transportation measures were struck down by state supreme courts.[6] *Everson* involved Ewing Township, New Jersey, a small community near Trenton which was too small to operate its own high school and therefore reimbursed parents for public bus transportation to schools in Trenton. Since parents who sent their children to parochial schools were reimbursed as well, the constitutionality of the state law that permitted reimbursement for nonpublic school transportation was challenged. The Supreme Court justices held unanimously that "no tax in any amount, large or small, can be levied to support any religious activities or institutions, whatever they may be called, or whatever form they may adopt, to teach or practice religion." However, by a five to four margin the Court upheld the reimbursement plan on the theory that the expenditure of public funds in this case was primarily for the public purpose of helping children get to school safely and expeditiously, even though there was some indirect benefit for the parochial school. For the majority Justice Black asserted that the plan approached the verge of the state's power but did not exceed it. Dissenting justices Wiley Rutledge and Robert Jackson argued that the plan crossed over the verge since it applied only to public and Catholic schools and not to other private schools or to children going elsewhere than to full-time day schools.

The *Everson* ruling upheld one state's transportation aid plan and indicated that such aid is discretionary, not mandatory. Since *Everson*, transportation aid has been considered by a number of state supreme courts. It has been ruled to be in violation of state constitutional provisions in Washington,[7] New Mexico,[8] Missouri,[9] Alaska,[10] Wisconsin,[11] Iowa,[12] Oklahoma,[13] Oregon,[14] and Hawaii,[15] and upheld in Connecticut,[16] Maine,[17] West Virginia,[18] and Pennsylvania.[19] Constitutional amendments to permit busing were approved in Wisconsin in 1966 and in Delaware in 1967, but defeated in referenda in Nebraska in 1966, in Idaho in 1972, and in Maryland in 1974.[20] On February 28, 1975, a New York appellate court ruled against the provision of public school buses for parochial school field trips.[21]

The lending of secular textbooks to parochial students has also been a troublesome issue for the courts. A Louisiana textbook loan program was upheld by the Supreme Court in 1930, but the statute was not challenged on First Amendment grounds.[22] Similar programs were found by state courts to violate state constitutions in New Mexico in 1951 and Oregon in 1962.[23] In 1968 the Supreme Court upheld New York's textbook loan program in *Board of Education* v. *Allen*, holding that the program benefitted children and not schools, that a loaned book is constitutionally the same as a bus ride, and that the statute setting up the plan had a secular purpose and a secular effect.[24] *Allen* may not have settled the issue, however. In 1973, in *Norwood* v. *Harrison*, the Supreme Court examined a Mississippi textbook loan plan and found neither *Allen* nor *Everson* dispositive. Since textbook loans "are a form of tangible financial assistance benefitting the schools themselves," the Court found it to be a violation of equal protection for the state to furnish textbooks to students in private schools that had racially discriminatory admissions policies.

The Court stated: "A state's constitutional obligation requires it to steer clear not only of operating the old dual system of racially segregated schools but also of giving significant aid to institutions that practice racial or other invidious discrimination."[25] Since parochial schools tend toward creedal homogeneity in their student bodies and faculties, are often segregated by sex, and are frequently out of balance racially when compared with neighboring public schools, *Norwood* may have paved the way for new and more sophisticated challenges to public aid for nonpublic schools.

In July 1983 the Kentucky Supreme Court ruled in *Fannin* v. *Williams* that a 1978 statute providing state subsidized textbooks for parochial schools violated the state constitution. The program, which became steadily more expensive, had allowed parochial schools to "borrow" state-approved "nonreligious" textbooks from the State Department of Libraries.[26]

THE MAJOR CASES

Advocates of parochiaid developed great political "clout" by the mid-1960s and succeeded in obtaining substantial benefits for parochial schools. Federal funding for some parochial school programs was included in the Elementary and Secondary Education Act passed by Congress in 1965. In the states, the *Allen* textbook ruling, with its seeming approval of the "child benefit" theory, opened the way for imaginative new parochiaid schemes. Pennsylvania began to "purchase secular educational services" from parochial and private schools. Rhode Island authorized state-paid supplements to the salaries of parochial teachers of secular subjects.

Taxpayers brought suits in both states. The Pennsylvania and Rhode Island suits, *Lemon* v. *Kurtzman* and *Earley* v. *Dicenso*,[27] were decided by the Supreme Court in a single opinion in 1971. Instead of following *Allen*, the Court relied on *Walz* v. *Tax Commission*,[28] a case dealing with property tax exemptions for church properties used for worship, and concluded that both the Rhode Island and Pennsylvania acts fostered an impermissible degree of entanglement between government and religion. The Court agreed with the Rhode Island federal district court decision that parochial schools constitute "an integral part of the religious mission of the Catholic

Church" and that the schools are "a powerful vehicle for transmitting the Catholic faith to the next generation." Both state legislatures, the Court said, had "recognized that church-related elementary and secondary schools have a significant religious mission and that a substantial portion of their activities are religiously oriented." While the legislatures "sought to create statutory restrictions designed to guarantee the separation between secular and religious educational functions and to insure that State financial aid supports only the former," the Court concluded that "the cumulative impact of the entire relationship arising under the statutes in each state involved excessive entanglement between government and religion.

One form of entanglement specifically feared by the Court in *Lemon* was the possibility that the state, in seeking to ensure that its funds would be used only for secular educational functions, would interfere too greatly in the operation of parochial schools. The Court recognized that "comprehensive, discriminating, and continuing state surveillance" would be required to restrict state aid to purely secular functions, and concluded that "these prophylactic contacts will involve excessive and enduring entanglement between church and state."

The Court also referred in *Lemon* to another type of entanglement which the First Amendment was intended to prevent:

> In a community where such a large number of pupils are served by church-related schools, it can be assumed that state assistance will entail considerable political activity. Partisans of parochial schools, understandably concerned with rising costs and sincerely dedicated to both the religious and secular educational missions of their schools, will inevitably champion this cause and promote political action to achieve their goals. Those who oppose state aid, whether for constitutional, religious, or fiscal reasons, will inevitably respond and employ all of the usual political campaign techniques to prevail. . . . Ordinarily political debate and division, however vigorous or even partisan, are normal and healthy manifestations of our democratic system of government, but political division along religious lines was one of the principal evils against which the First Amendment was intended to protect.[29]

Two days after the *Lemon* decision the Court affirmed a federal district court decision striking down a similar Connecticut plan.[30]

After *Lemon* new aid plans continued to move from the drawing boards, through state legislatures, across governors' desks, and finally into the courts. In 1970 the New York legislature enacted a program in which the state paid nonpublic schools for "mandated services," services such as keeping records and conducting examinations which are required by the state of all schools.[31] In 1972 New York passed another act to assist parochial and private schools through "health and safety" grants for building repair and maintenance, tuition reimbursement grants to low-income parents, and a sort of state income tax credit for parochial parents of moderate income.[32] In 1971 Ohio and Pennsylvania passed tuition reimbursement plans.[33] After a federal district court struck down the Ohio reimbursement plan in April 1972, the legislature enacted a tax-credit tuition reimbursement plan in June 1972, which in turn was challenged in federal court.[34] The Supreme Court handed down a brace of rulings on these plans on June 25, 1973.

In *Committee for Public Education and Religious Liberty* v. *Nyquist*,[35] the Supreme Court held that the New York "health and safety" grants violated the Establishment Clause because their effect was to "subsidize and advance the mission of sectarian schools." Similarly, both the New York tuition reimbursement grants and tax credit tuition reimbursements were held to "have the impermissible effect of advancing religion." In *Leavitt* v. *Committee for Public Education and Religious Liberty*,[36] New York's "mandated services" funding program was found to be unconstitutional because the law provided no means to assure that aid would not go to sectarian activities. In *Sloan* v. *Lemon*[37] the Court struck down Pennsylvania's tuition reimbursement plan as being constitutionally indistinguishable from the New York plan.

Ohio's tuition reimbursement and tax credit plans were found to be unconstitutional by a federal district court in 1972, and the ruling was affirmed by the Suprme Court.[38] Subsequently, a California federal court[39] and the Minnesota Supreme Court[40] struck down those states' tax credit parochiaid plans. Ambitious plans to have Congress enact a $1 billion federal tax credit tuition reimbursement program died quietly after the Supreme Court's 1973 rulings.

In other developments, a Vermont federal court in 1972 ruled unconstitutional a state law under which teachers and educational materials were "lent" to parochial and private schools. The plan was held to create an excessive entanglement between religion and government and also to create a potential for the impermissible fostering of religion.[41] In 1973 a New Hampshire federal court ruled against a parochiaid plan sometimes called "reverse shared time" (see chapter 4). The district court held that the plan went beyond mere "excessive entanglement" to become a merger of church and state.[42] A similiar Kentucky plan was found unconstitutional in 1974.[43]

New Jersey enacted a plan to reimburse parochial and private school parents for the cost of secular textbooks, instructional materials, and supplies, with any money left over from the program to be assigned to nonpublic schools for the acquisition of secular supplies, equipment, and auxiliary services. A federal court in 1973 held that, since the program was limited to parents of children attending only predominantly sectarian private schools and excluded public school parents, it had the unconstitutional primary effect of advancing religion. Lending equipment and providing auxiliary services personnel to parochial schools was held to create the potential for excessive church-state entanglement. The ruling was affirmed by the Supreme Court in 1974.

Both the Pennsylvania and Ohio legislatures enacted programs to aid parochial schools through the lending of textbooks and instructional equipment and materials and the provision of publicly paid personnel for such "auxiliary services" as guidance, testing, and remedial teaching. Lower federal courts in the two states upheld the plans in 1974, but both decisions were reversed by the Supreme Court in 1975.[44] The Court held that the equipment and material loans had the unconstitutional effect of providing direct and substantial state aid in advancement of a religious activity. The "auxiliary services" were held to violate the First Amendment because they "necessarily give rise to a constitutionally intolerable degree of entanglement between church and state." The Court followed the 1968 *Allen* precedent, however, in holding the textbook loans to be constitutional.[45]

A novel approach to the parochiaid problem was taken in Missouri by parochial school parents who asked the federal courts to rule that their rights under the First and Fourteenth Amendments were violated by provisions of the Missouri constitution strictly forbidding public aid for nonpublic schools. A lower federal court ruled against the plaintiffs and the Supreme Court affirmed the decision without opinion in 1972.[46]

In 1973 the Supreme Court struck down New York's Chapter 138, which provided for state reimbursement to private schools for state-mandated services. The five to four majority held that the program unconstitutionally aided religion because there was no provision to identify and separate sectarian functions from secular ones in church-related schools.[47]

The following year found two more separationist rulings from the nation's highest court. In the *Franchise Tax Board of California* case[48] the Court affirmed without written opinion a federal district court decision invalidating state income tax deductions for parents who utilize parochial schools. In *Leutkemeyer* v. *Kaufmann*[49] the Court affirmed a Missouri federal court's decision that the state constitution prohibited public financing of parochial school bus transportation. This decision is significant because the Supreme Court said that a state constitution's prohibitions against parochiaid may be upheld even if the federal constitution were held to allow certain kinds of aid, as in *Everson*. The Missouri court had ruled that "the Constitution of the United States does not compel the state of Missouri to provide equal transportation services to private and church-sponsored schools."[50]

The Court began to weaken slightly in 1977's complicated *Wolman* v. *Walters* decision. This time the justices upheld parts of an Ohio law designed to aid parochial schools. The approved textbooks, testing and scoring services, diagnostic services, therapeutic and remedial services, and instructional materials and equipment. They disallowed field trips and the supplying of projectors, maps, globes, and other instructional equipment which were not loaned to parents and students. The Court held that most of the allowable programs could be held at neutral sites, away from the "pervasively sectarian atmosphere of the church-related school," while field trips would be under the direction of the schools and could easily be transformed into religious education.[51]

In 1979 the Court struck down a New Jersey law that provided a tax deduction of $1,000 per child for parents with children in religious schools. The six to three decision held the plan unconstitutional because it advanced religion impermissibly.[52]

The next decision signaled a weakening of the separationist line. In *PEARL* v. *Regan*[53] the Court took a second look at a New York law that allowed lump sum payments to private and religious schools for the actual cost of state-mandated testing and reporting services. This included administrative costs of state-prepared and required examinations, the preparation of school enrollment and attendance data, the auditing of payments, and the verfication of services. After the *Levitt* ruling of 1973 invalidated the scheme, New York legislators restricted payments to grading of state-prepared examinations, which concerned only secular subjects. This time, by a five to four margin, the justices reversed themselves and upheld the New York law. Justice Byron White, writing for the majority, even suggested that the three-part *Lemon* test was elusive and not an impeccable standard for evaluating church-state case law, a view espoused by the Bush administration in 1991.

Separationists shuddered even more when the *Mueller* v. *Allen*[54] ruling came down in 1983. At issue was a Minnesota law allowing all parents with children in tuition-charging schools to deduct expenses for tuition, textbooks, and transportation from their state income tax. The statute allowed a $500 per child deduction from grades kindergarten through six, and $700 per pupil for grades seven through twelve. (While it will be obvious to most, it should be noted that a tax deduction involves far less money than a tax credit. A deduction lowers taxable income, while a credit lowers the tax itself and has the effect of transferring a much larger amount of money to the school.) Both the district court and the Eighth Circuit Court of Appeals upheld the law and rejected the taxpayers' claims that the act violated the First Amendment by advancing religion.[55]

Justice William Rehnquist, writing for the five to four majority, said that because the deduction was available to *all* parents in *all* kinds of schools, the church-state problem was avoided. The majority denied that the law had a primary effect of advancing religion. They also held that the law did not create excessive entanglement between church and state because there was no interaction between parents and state officials. The law did require that state officials would have to choose which textbooks qualified for the deduction. The cost of religion textbooks could not be deducted.

In a stinging dissent Justice Thurgood Marshall, joined by three colleagues, insisted that the Minnesota statute "subsidizes tuition payments to sectarian schools."[56] Marshall and his colleagues were particularly indignant over the fact that the majority ruling ignored the finding that 96 percent of the beneficiaries of the law attended church-related schools, since very few public schools charge tuition. The dissenters argued, "A tax deduction has a primary effect that advances religion if it is provided to offset expenditures which are not restricted to the secular activities of parochial schools."[57] The dissent also scoffed at the supposedly antiseptic textbook provision, saying, "Secular textbooks, like other secular instructional materials, contribute to the religious mission of the parochial school that uses those books."[58] Marshall concluded that the *Mueller* ruling "is flatly at odds with the fundamental principle that a state may provide no financial support whatsoever to promote religion."[59]

The *Mueller* ruling remains the single most pro-parochiaid decision since *Everson*. Bryson and Houston thought *Mueller* was "the most important decision affecting public and religious schools" issued by the Burger Court.[60] They suggested that "*Mueller* has the potential to establish two public-funded school systems in America: a public education system, with unchurched, minority, handicapped, and indigent students enrolled; and a religious schools system, with almost all white students."[61]

That this has not occurred may be due to the brake applied in 1985 by a more cautious Supreme Court in *Grand Rapids School District* v. *Ball*.[62] In this decision a five to four majority, led by William J. Brennan, the grand old man of church-state separation, ruled that the Grand Rapids shared time and community education program held on religious school property was unconstitutional.

Robert T. Miller and Ronald B. Flowers commented on this decision in the following discussion: "The plan in *Grand Rapids* was found to have the primary effect of advancing religion in three ways: (1) the state-paid teachers, working in a sectarian environment, might indoctrinate students in religion; (2) the fact of state-paid teachers working in parochial schools symbolically conveys the message of state-support of religion; and (3) the programs effectively subsidize religion by assuming a portion of the parochial school's responsibility for teaching secular subjects."[63]

In this crisply worded decision, Justice Brennan summarized the heart of the separationist argument:

> Providing for the education of schoolchildren is surely a praiseworthy purpose. But our cases have consistently recognized that even such a praiseworthy, secular purpose cannot validate government aid to parochial schools when the aid has the effect of promoting a single religion or religion generally or when the aid unduly entangles the government in matters religious. For just as religion throughout history

has provided spiritual comfort, guidance, and inspiration to many, it can also serve powerfully to divide societies and to exclude those whose beliefs are not in accord with particular religions or sects that have from time to time achieved dominance. The solution to this problem adopted by the Framers and consistently recognized by this Court is jealously to guard the right of every individual to worship according to the dictates of conscience while requiring the government to maintain a course of neutrality among religions, and between religion and nonreligion.[64]

Brennan added: "Our cases have recognized that the Establishment Clause guards against more than direct, state-funded efforts to indoctrinate youngsters in specific religious beliefs. Government promotes religions as effectively when it fosters a close identification of its powers and responsibilities with those of any—or all—religious denominations as when it attempts to inculcate specific religious doctrines. If this identification conveys a message of government endorsement or disapproval of religion, a core purpose of the Establishment Clause is violated."[65]

This is where the parochiaid controversy remains after forty years of not wholly consistent Supreme Court decisions. It is not always easy to understand the Court's occasional twists and turns in this thicket, but Professors Miller and Flowers sum up the trends in this way:

In summary, decisions of the Supreme Court indicate that certain kinds of state aid may be made available to parochial schools: bus transportation, textbook loans, and services for the educational health and welfare of the student, so long as it is manifestly clear that the performance of these services is absolutely secular. This secularity requirement is easily seen by comparing *Meek* and *Wolman.* Because the parochial school is an arm of the church and its principal purpose is the instruction of children in the church's doctrine and the advancement of its religious mission, any other forms of aid which would contribute to this cause have been declared unconstitutional. As a result of *Mueller,* government aid may be given to church-related schools by means of tuition supplements through tax deductions for parents sending children to such schools, provided that the deductions are available to parents of children going to any kind of school, i.e., the tax deductions must be applicable to educational expenses across the board. On the other hand, when it comes to the financing of particular educational activities within parochial schools, the negative decisions in *Grand Rapids* and *Felton* mean that *Wolman* still sets the boundaries of what is permissible.[66]

NOTES

1. Edd Doerr, *The Conspiracy That Failed* (Silver Springs, Md.: Americans United, 1968), pp. 17–27; Leo Pfeffer, *Church, State, and Freedom* (Boston: Beacon Press, 1967), pp. 530–33.

2. Ellwood P. Cubberley, *The History of Education* (New York: Houghton Mifflin, 1948), pp. 530–33.

3. Pfeffer, *Church, State, and Freedom*, pp. 537–54. *Harfst* v. *Hoegen*, 349 Mo. 808, 163 S.W. 2d 609 (1942); *Zellers* v. *Huff*, 55 N.M. 501, 236 P. 2d 949 (1951).

4. *Flast* v. *Cohen*, 392 U.S. 83 (1968).

5. 330 U.S. 1 (1947).

6. *State ex rel. Traub* v. *Brown*, 36 Del. 181 (1934); *Gurney* v. *Ferguson*, 190 Okla. 254 (1941); *Judd* v. *Board of Education*, 278 NY 200 (1938); *Mitchell* v. *Consolidated School District*, 17 Washington 2d 61 (1943).

7. *Visser* v. *Nooksack Valley School District*, 33 Washington 2d 699 (1949).

8. *Zellers* v. *Huff*, 55 N.M. 501 (1951).

9. *McVey* v. *Hawkins*, 258 S.W. 2d 927 (o., 1953).

10. *Matthews* v. *Quinton*, 362 P. 2d 932 (Alaska, 1961).

11. *Reynolds* v. *Nussbaum*, 115 N.W. 761 (Wisc., 1962).

12. *Silver Lake School District* v. *Barker*, 29 N.W. 2d 214 (Iowa, 1947).

13. *Board of Education* v. *Antone*, 384 P. 2d 911 (Okla., 1963).

14. *Dickman* v. *Oregon School District*, 366 P. 2nd 533 (1961).

15. *Spears* v. *Honda*, 51 Ha. 1 (1968).

16. *Snyder* v. *Newton*, 161 A. 2d 770 (Conn., 1961).

17. *Squires* v. *City of Augusta*, 155 Me 151 (1959).

18. *Hughes* v. *Board of Education of the County of Kanawha*, 154 W. Va. 107 Vol 174 S.E. 2nd 711 (1970).

19. *Rhoades* v. *School District of Abington County*, 424 Pa 202, Vol. 226 At. 2d 53 (1967).

20. *Church & State*, vols. 20 (January 1967: 8; June 1967: 4–5), 21 (April 1968: 10), 25 (December 1972: 3), and 27 (December 1974: 3).

21. *Cook* v. *Hamburg Central School District*, Appellate Division of the Supreme Court. 4th Department, New York (1975).

22. *Cochran* v. *Louisiana State Board of Education*, 281 U.S. 370 (1930).

23. *Zellers* v. *Huff*, 55 N.M. 501 (1951); *Dickman* v. *Oregon School*

District, 366 P. 2d 533, certiorari den. 371 U.S. 823 (1962).

24. *Board of Education* v. *Allen*, 392 U.S. 236 (1968).

25. *Norwood* v. *Harrison*, 93 S.Ct. 2804 (1973).

26. "Kentucky Supreme Court Halts Textbook Subsidy for Parochial Schools," *Church & State* 36 (September 1983): 19–20.

27. 403 U.S. 602 (1971).

28. 397 U.S. 664 (1970).

29. 403 U.S. 602 (1971).

30. *Sanders* v. *Johnson*, DC 319 F. Supp. 421, 403 U.S. 955 (1971).

31. "Rocky Strikes Again," *Church & State* 23 (July–August 1970): 70.

32. "New York Does It Again," *Church & State* 25 (July–August 1972): 3.

33. "Rebound in Pennsylvania," *Church & State* 24 (October 1971): 3; "New Ohio Parochiaid Law Challenged," *Church & State* 25 (February 1972): 3.

34. "Parochiaid's Days of Judgment," *Church & State* 25 (September 1972): 10–12.

35. 413 US 756 (1973).

36. 413 US 472 (1973).

37. 413 US 825 (1973).

38. *Wolman* v. *Essex*, 342 F. Supp. 399, 419, 409 U.S. 808 (1972); *Kosyder* v. *Wolman*, (*Grit* v. *Wolman*) 353 F. Supp. 744, 413 U.S. 901 (1973).

39. *United Americans* v. *Francis Tax Board*, 43 U.S. Law Week 3231 (1974).

40. *Minnesota Civil Liberties Union* v. *Minnesota*, 224 NW 2nd 344 (1974).

41. *Americans United* v. *Oakey*, 339 F. Supp. 545 (1972).

42. *Americans United* v. *Paire*, 359 F. Supp. 505 (1973).

43. *Americans United* v. *Beechwood School District*, 369 F. Supp. 1059 (1974).

44. *Meek* v. *Pittenger*, 374 F. supp. 639 (1974), 421 US 349 (1975); *Wolman* v. *Essex and Needle*, 342 F. Supp. 399 (1974), reversed and remanded May 27, 1975.

45. Ibid.

46. *Brusca* v. *State of Missouri*, 332 F. Supp. 275, 405 U.S. 1050 (1972).

47. *Cathedral Academy* v. *PEARL*, 413 US 37 (1973).

48. 419 US 890 (1974).

49. 419 US 888 (1974).

50. 364 F. Supp. 378 (W.D. Mo. 1973).

51. 433 US 229 (1977).

52. *Byrne* v. *Public Funds for Public Schools of New Jersey*, 442 US 907 (1979).

53. 444 US 646 (1980).

54. 463 US 388 (1983).

55. 514 F. Supp. 998 (D. Minn 1981).

56. 463 US 404.

57. 463 US 414.

58. Ibid.

59. 463 US 417.

60. Joseph Bryson and Samuel Houston, *The Supreme Court and Public Funds for Religious Schools* (Jefferson, N.C.: McFarland & Co., 1990), p. 110.

61. Ibid., p. 129.

62. 473 US 373.

63. Robert T. Miller and Ronald B. Flowers, *Toward Benevolent Neutrality: Church, State, and the Supreme Court* (Waco, Tex.: Markham Press Fund of Baylor University Press, 1987), p. 457.

64. 473 US 373.

65. Ibid.

66. Miller and Flowers, *Toward Benevolent Neutrality*, p. 458.

8

Parochiaid: Pro and Con

Debate over tax aid or to support of nonpublic schools has waxed and waned in our country for over a century and a half, just as it has in Canada, Australia, the United Kingdom, France, Belgium, the Netherlands, Spain, and other countries. In this chapter we will examine the principal arguments for and against parochiaid in any form.

SCHOOL CHOICE

Educational choice is the buzzword of the 1990s in the controversy over parochiaid. If only parents could choose their children's schools, the argument runs, competition among schools would provide the carrots and sticks to improve all education. Bad or ineffective schools would either get better and attract students or else wither and eventually go out of business.

Choice, of course, is a good word, an excellent word. It resonates favorably with nearly everyone. People favor choice when it comes to careers, spouses, friends, elections, religion, entertainment, cars, and toothpaste. It is the key word in that other important church-state controversy, whether or not women should have the legal/constitutional right to freedom of conscience on abortion.

Choice in the school context means many different things. It certainly refers to the smorgasbord of course choices available to most students in our comprehensive public high schools, choices made possible in large measure because public high schools generally have enough students to permit the offering of a wide variety of courses. Nonpublic high schools, which generally serve much smaller student bodies, are rarely able to offer as many courses. School choice may also refer to choice among public schools within a particular school district or to choices among public schools in several districts or possibly even a whole state. Finally, choice may be extended to nonpublic schools, as is being advocated by President Bush, the Catholic bishops, certain televangelists and fundamentalist leaders, and the authors of the book *Politics, Markets, and America's Schools.*[1]

As applied to nonpublic schools, over 90 percent of which are sectarian religious institutions, tax-funded choice is clearly improper and unwise public policy, as we will show in detail elsewhere in this chapter.

But before doing so, we note a serious flaw and a conscious deception in the rhetoric of those who use the choice argument to get tax support for nonpublic schools. Promoters of choice plans that go beyond public schools talk about families choosing schools for their children. But they are putting the cart before the horse. Families may *apply* to have their children admitted to a nonpublic school, but it is the nonpublic schools that really do the choosing. They choose which students to admit or retain and which to reject or expel, which teachers to hire and which to reject, and which religion or ideology will permeate the school program. Now many of these schools want to choose tax support for themselves expressly by denying taxpayers the right to choose which religious institutions they, the taxpayers, will support.

Those who advocate including nonpublic schools in tax-funded choice plans offer choice as a panacea, but do not offer specific proposals for improving the programs of existing schools.

CONSTITUTIONALITY

Tax aid for religious elementary and secondary schools has generally been found by federal and state courts to violate the U.S. and state constitutions, except for what some might regard as minor and peripheral forms of tax aid (see chapter 7). The Constitution means what the Supreme Court says it means, however, and parochiaid advocates have expressed confidence that some of the newer justices on the Court could tip the Court's balance and weaken or overturn some of the Court's previous rulings against parochiaid. Civil libertarians and church-state separationists fear that this could happen, and thus remind concerned citizens that the Supreme Court may not continue to be the great protector of fundamental rights that many people had come to count on.

There are two basic schools of thought with regard to the constitutionality of parochiaid. The church-state separationist position, to which the authors of this volume adhere, is essentially the position that the Supreme Court has repeatedly affirmed since its first major establishment clause ruling in *Everson* in 1947, namely, that all but the most peripheral forms of tax aid to religious institutions are unconstitutional. The most concise expression of that position is to be found in the following quotations from the majority and dissenting opinions in *Everson* by Justices Hugo L. Black and Wiley Rutledge.

Justice Black wrote:

The "establishment of religion" clause of the First Amendment means at least this: Neither a state nor the Federal Government can set up a church. Neither can pass laws which aid one religion, aid all religions, or prefer one religion over another. Neither can force nor influence a person to go to or to remain away from church against his will or force him to profess a belief or disbelief in any religion. No person can be punished for entertaining or professing religious beliefs or disbeliefs, for church attendance or nonattendance. No tax in any amount, large or small, can be levied to support any religious activities or institutions, whatever they may be called, or whatever form they may adopt to teach or practice religion. Neither a state or the Federal Government can, openly or secretly, participate in the affairs of any religious organizations or groups and vice versa. In the words of Jefferson, the clause against establishment of religion by law was intended to erect "a wall of separation between church and state. . . ."[2] That wall must be kept high and impregnable. We could not approve the slightest breach.[3]

Justice Rutledge stated: "The [First] Amendment's purpose was not to strike merely at the official establishment of a single sect, creed, or religion, outlawing only a formal relation such as had prevailed in England and some of the colonies. Necessarily it was to uproot all such relationships. But the object was broader than separating church and state in this narrow sense. It was to create a complete and permanent separation of the spheres of religious activity and civil authority by comprehensively forbidding every form of public aid or support for religion."[4]

Rutledge concluded that, "[w]e have staked the very existence of our country on the faith that a complete separation between the state and religion is best for the state and best for religion.[5]. . . The Constitution requires not comprehensive identification of state with religion, but complete separation."[6]

The separationist position has generally been supported by Americans for Religious Liberty, the American Civil Liberties Union, the many groups in the National Coalition for Public Education and Religious Liberty, public education and PTA groups, religious groups such as the Baptist Joint Committee on Public Affairs, the United Methodist Church, the Unitarian Universalist Association, and most Jewish groups. With regard to parochiaid, the separationist view has been upheld by nearly every statewide electorate that has had a chance to vote directly on the issue during the past quarter-century (see chapter 5).

In contrast to the separationist position is what has come to be referred to as the "accommodationist" position. It has been espoused by Chief Justice William Rehnquist, Presidents Reagan and Bush, the Catholic bishops, a number of fundamentalist leaders, and writers who advocate the privatization of education. According to accommodationists, the First Amendment was intended neither to erect what Jefferson in 1802 called the "wall of separation between church and state" nor to bar all government aid to religion, but rather to allow "nonpreferential" government aid to all religions. Chief Justice Rehnquist, in his dissenting opinion in *Wallace* v. *Jaffree*,[7] referred to the separationist view as "an historically faulty doctrine," and insisted that the First Amendment framers sought only "to prohibit the designation of any church as a 'national' one" and to "stop the Federal Government from asserting a preference for one religious denomination or sect over others."

It is the accommodationist position, however, that is flawed.

When the First Amendment was being drafted in 1789, there was little fear of a European-style or early colonial-style single establishment of religion being set up on either the national or state level. Constitutional historian C. Herman Pritchett explains this well:

The phrase "establishment of religion" must be given the meaning that it had in the United States in 1791, rather than its European connotation. In America there was no establishment of a single church, as in England. Four states had never adopted any establishment practices. They had abolished their establishments during the Revolution. The remaining six states—Massachusetts, New Hampshire, Connecticut, Maryland, South Carolina, and Georgia—changed to comprehensive or "multiple" establishments. That is, aid was provided to all churches in each state on a nonpreferential basis, except that the establishment was limited to churches of the Protestant religion in three states and to those of the Christian religion in the other three states. Since there were almost no Catholics in the first group of states, and very few Jews in any state, this meant that the multiple establishment practices included every religious group with enough members to form a church. It was this nonpreferential assistance to organized churches that constituted "establishment of religion" in 1791 and it was this practice that the Amendment forbade Congress to adopt."[8]

Further, as John M. Swomley, theologian and president of Americans for Religious Liberty, points out, Congress, in developing the language of the First Amendment, specifically rejected the accommodationist or nonpreferentialist view. The formulations rejected by Congress were "Congress shall make no law establishing one religious sect or society in preference to others," "Congress shall not make any law . . . establishing any religious sect or society," and "Congress shall make no law establishing any particular denomination or religion in preference to another." When Senate and House conferees, including Madison, met to finalize the First Amendment, they agreed on the present wording, "Congress shall make no law respecting an establishment of religion, or prohibiting the free exercise thereof." The first Congress, therefore, adopted First Amendment language far broader and more restrictive than that congenial to the accommodationists and nonpreferentialists of that day or this.[9]

Swomley adds: "It would be illogical to suppose that an amendment expressly designed to prohibit a power never given to Congress in the Constitution should be construed as creating the authority to enact laws benefitting religion financially. Yet this is precisely what contemporary proponents of aid to churches are trying to do."[10]

The separationist position is further supported when it is noted that the drafting and ratification of the Constitution, which implicitly supports separation of church and state by not granting the federal government any authority whatever to promote any or all religions, and the Bill of Rights, occurred immediately after the struggle in Virginia. This campaign was led by James Madison, chief architect of the Constitution and Bill of Rights, to defeat Patrick Henry's non-preferentialist bill for providing tax aid to all religions and to pass Jefferson's Bill for Establishing Religious Freedom, which barred any tax for "any religious worship, place, or ministry whatsoever."

DOLLAR COSTS

Including nonpublic schools in tax-funded school choice plans will entail extremely high costs for taxpayers.

Adding to the costs of operating existing nonpublic schools to those of public schools will obviously increase elementary and secondary school costs across the nation by at least ten percent, as the number of students in tax-supported schools rises by at least ten percent.

Parochiaid advocates may object to that figure on the ground that many nonpublic schools operate at lower per-student costs than public schools. Where that is true, it occurs because nonpublic schools pay teachers less, offer fewer educational services (such as expensive vocational courses, counseling and guidance, language labs, etc.), and serve a far lower percentage of handicapped children than public schools. Public schools, unlike nonpublic, are required to provide equal educational services for handicapped children, which may cost five or six times as much per student as the education of nonhandicapped children. If nonpublic schools were required to offer the same salaries and same level of services as public schools, their per-student costs would be at least as high. In addition, tax-funded nonpublic schools would probably have higher per-student costs because, having smaller enrollments, they would be less likely than public schools to be able to take advantage of economies of scale.

A separate but related factor must also be considered, and that lies in the matter of school busing and the choice of schools.

Transportation costs are a further complicating factor in tax-funded choice programs, whether confined to public schools or not. About half of all public students are bused to school, either because the schools are too far away for walking or because students would have to cross dangerous streets and highways. If students were allowed to go to the public school of their choice within their own school district, obviously a much larger percentage of students would have to be bused, and busing costs would increase proportionately. If students could attend public schools in other districts, as some choice plans would allow, transportation costs would go still higher. If nonpublic schools are included in choice plans, busing costs would rise astronomically. Pennsylvania already requires that students be bused to nonpublic schools miles outside their public school districts and even across state lines into Ohio, Delaware, and New Jersey, at enormous cost to hard-pressed public school districts. Howard County, Maryland, buses students to five church schools within the county (which in Maryland is coterminous with the school district); it costs precisely twice as much to bus a student to a church school as to a public school. In northern Ohio, a school district is required to transport two students *by airplane and taxi* from an island in Lake Erie to a church school on the mainland, even though the island has its own public schools; the transportation alone for the students costs more than Ohio spends per year educating a student.

Who will pay for the transportation to "schools of choice"? If the taxpayers pick up the bill, the costs will be enormous, and this at a time when states and cities from coast to coast are being forced to slash school budgets, cut programs, increase class sizes, lay off teachers, and freeze salaries. If the public does not pay the transportation bills for getting students to schools of choice, then only children whose parents can drive them to school will be served. Choice plans, whether they include nonpublic schools or not, would surely add to school administrative complexity and costs overall.

With public school budgets either static or shrinking in most of the country's nearly 16,000 school districts, choice plans, with or without the inclusion of nonpublic schools, must either be paid for by raising taxes or cutting back on existing public school budgets. Our public schools need more money if they are to attract good teachers, fully fund Head Start and other vitally important programs, repair and/or replace crumbling school buildings in many cities, and extend the present 180-day school year to catch up with the longer school years of some of our international competitors like Germany and Japan.

A TAX FOR RELIGION

Of all the arguments against any kind of parochiaid, under whatever guise, perhaps the most cogent and simple is this: It is wrong for government to compel people through taxation to contribute to the support of religious teachings, programs, or institutions which they do not individually choose to support voluntarily. Over 90 percent of nonpublic enrollment is in schools operated as independent institutions primarily for denominational religious purposes, in which curricula are permeated by a denominational point of view (see chapter 3).

Thomas Jefferson put it eloquently in his Bill for Establishing Religious Freedom, passed by the Virginia legislature in 1786: "[T]o compel a man to furnish contributions of money for the propagation of opinions which he disbelieves and abhors, is sinful and tyrannical; . . . even the forcing him to support this or that teacher of his own religious persuasion, is depriving him of the comfortable liberty of giving his contributions to the particular pastor whose morals he would make his pattern, and whose powers he feels most persuasive to righteousness." There is no more basic American principle than that all individuals be free to support only those religious institutions or enterprises they wish to support.

A distinguished contemporary religious liberty leader, Florence Flast, vice-chair of the National Coalition for Public Education and Religious Liberty, put it well: "Religious liberty in America means not only the right to pursue one's own beliefs, but freedom from compulsory taxation to foster the religious beliefs of others."[11]

The Episcopal weekly, *The Living Church*, echoed these views: "Christians who care enough about their faith to want it properly taught to their children in the course of their education should care enough to pay for it, however heavy the burden. . . . When any of our tax money is used, directly or indirectly, to subsidize any religious teaching without our consent, government is coercing us in this realm where coercion does not belong."[12]

The United Methodist Church adopted a resolution at its 1980 General Assembly which expresses the convictions of millions of thoughtful Americans: "We specifically oppose tuition tax credits or any other mechanism which directly or indirectly allows government funds to support religious schools at the primary and secondary level.

Persons of one particular faith should be free to use their own funds to strengthen the belief system of their particular religious group. But they should not expect all taxpayers, including those who adhere to other religious beliefs systems, to provide funds to teach religious views with which they do not agree. . . ."

TAXATION WITHOUT REPRESENTATION

One of the rallying cries during the period immediately prior to the American Revolution was "Taxation without representation is tyranny!" In other words, in a country in which government is supposed to be "of the people, by the people, and for the people," the people should control, through democratic machinery, what they have to pay for.

The sectarian and other special interests seeking tax support for nonpublic schools really do not want the public to control and regulate what they are being asked to pay for, for that would surely eliminate all or most of what differentiates nonpublic from public schools. If tax-supported nonpublic schools had to play by the same rules as the public schools, they could no longer offer denominational teaching or apply admissions or hiring standards different from those of public schools.

If boards representing the whole taxpaying public exercise meaningful control over any nonpublic schools that receive public funding, in the vast majority of cases the adherents to the faith groups that originally operated the school will be in a small minority.

SOCIAL FRAGMENTATION

Only slightly over ten percent of our children are enrolled in nonpublic elementary and secondary schools. Tax support for nonpublic schools could only cause the nonpublic sector to grow. This, in turn, would inevitably increase social fragmentation along religious, social class, and other lines, producing a society much less able than it is at present to cope with the country's growing problems.

As we saw in chapter 2, the most important characteristic of nonpublic schools is their pervasively religious nature. Parochiaid on a massive scale, then, would further divide our society along religious lines.

Because nonpublic schools, especially on the secondary level, tend to be academically selective and tend to enroll children of families with average incomes considerably higher than those of public school students, parochiaid will increase social division along class lines. This in turn is likely to increase ethnic division, as the average incomes of white families are considerably higher than those of African Americans, Native Americans, and Hispanic Americans. James S. Catterall, a specialist in school finance issues, found that tax aid to private schools would disproportionately favor the well-off at every level of society. For example, only 3.2 percent of families at the lowest income level send their children to nonpublic schools, compared to 16.5 percent of families at the highest income level.[13]

Nonpublic schools are not required to serve handicapped students, and a far lower percentage of nonpublic students are handicapped compared to public school enrollments. There is also a racial imbalance. Catterall writes: "Blacks account for about 15 percent of all elementary school enrollments and for only about 8 percent of private elementary school enrollments. Blacks in high schools account for 13.5 percent of total enrollments and 6 percent of private enrollments."[14]

Perhaps the most serious difference between public and private schools is the amount of time and energy devoted to students with special needs, such as the handicapped and visually impaired. Here the difference is striking. As Catterall notes: "In general private schools do not provide the high-cost programs for special-need pupils. Only about 2.7 percent of church-affiliated schools provide programs for the handicapped; only 3 percent of all nonpublic schools provide vocational education; and about 4.4 percent provide compensatory education."[15]

Given the forms of selectivity common in nonpublic schools, it would not take much of an increase in nonpublic enrollment—say, to 20 percent or so of the school population—to split our school population into privileged enclaves for the fortunate few and a large public, separate but unequal system for the poor, the handicapped, the "slow," ethnic minorities, and the children who are rejected by or ejected from the nonpublic school sector.

Since political influence tends to be proportional to income and educational level, massive parochiaid would tend to shrink the effective political clout of those whose children attend public schools and expand the influence of the privileged minority whose children attend nonpublic schools.

POLITICAL DIVISIVENESS

Both attempts to legalize parochiaid and the success of those attempts inevitably mean great political divisiveness along religious lines, precisely one of the evils that the First Amendment was designed to prevent, if we may paraphrase the U.S. Supreme Court in its *Lemon* v. *Kurtzman* ruling. As we have shown, this issue—more than any other—has a passion and a continuity that continually divide U.S. religious groups into warring camps.

Inevitably, religious communities will struggle to compete at the legislative trough for greater and greater funding of their schools. More numerically powerful and politically sophisticated religions will thrive at the expense of weaker ones. The ecumenical spirit, which emphasizes common goals and concerns of benefit to the entire community, will suffer—as it has already suffered repeatedly in the parochiaid battles of the past.

The danger to the American body politic is incalculable. Religion will become a greater wedge in political disputes and will be seen as a threatening, politically manipulated force. Religious lobbies will establish themselves as separate interest groups and political blocs, further fragmenting the electorate. This has already happened in state capitals and in Washington, D.C., where increasingly powerful religious lobbies dot the landscape. This trend, if left unchecked, can only harm interfaith concord. It may also damage working relationships between religious organizations and governmental bodies.

Justice Wiley Rutledge, in his dissent in the 1947 *Everson* ruling, expressed these fears well: "Public money devoted to payment of religious cost, educational or other, brings the quest for more. It brings, too, the struggle of sect against sect for the larger share or for any. . . . That is precisely the history of societies which have had an established religion and dissident groups. It is the very thing Jefferson and Madison experienced and sought to guard against, whether in its blunt or in its more screened forms. The end of such strife cannot be other than to destroy the cherished liberty. . . ."[16]

Justice John Marshall Harlan expressed a similar view: "The First Amendment's prohibition against governmental establishment of religion was written on the assumption that state aid to religion and religious schools generates discord, disharmony, hatred, and strife among our people, and that any government that supplies such aids is to that extent a tyranny."[17]

Many American Catholics have been offended and embarrassed by official church involvement in parochiaid politics. In New York's 1967 constitutional referendum battle, for example, church leaders hired an expensive Madison Avenue advertising firm, carried on voter registration drives in churches, used the diocesan press and church-run television facilities, sponsored a huge political rally at Madison Square Garden, and required the reading of political statements from all pulpits on the Sunday prior to the election. The politicization of religion offended churchgoers of all political persuasions.

The national Catholic journal, *Commonweal*, in its October 20, 1967, issue, editorialized sharply: "The inevitable conclusion is that Catholic interest in the constitution is selfish and determined by the opportunities the new constitution would open up in the way of aid to Catholic schools."

The campaign's religious divisiveness led the liberal Protestant weekly *Christianity and Crisis*, which favored parochiaid, to state editorially: "What we see in New York is a Catholic power play of the type associated with pre-conciliar Catholicism. As a result we are both dismayed and chagrined."[18]

TEACHERS' INTERESTS

Teachers are obviously the key to good education. And teaching has become a modestly attractive profession largely because teacher organizations, such as the local groups of the National Education Association and the American Federation of Teachers, have been able to get better salaries, working conditions, pensions, academic freedom, and freedom from arbitrary dismissal through collective bargaining. Nonpublic teachers usually do not have effective collective bargaining units or the other advantages of public school teachers, though some nonpublic teachers enjoy the advantage of teaching only selected, academically privileged students and some people are able to find positions in nonpublic schools when they lack the training and credentials for teaching in public schools.

Voucherization and privatization of education would most probably reduce academic freedom, degrade teaching as a profession, lower teacher standards, and greatly reduce job stability. After all, it is not uncommon for church school teachers to be fired or not hired because of their religious beliefs, their stands on social issues, or their marital status.

WOMEN'S RIGHTS

Tax support for nonpublic schools poses serious threats to women's rights. The overwhelming majority of nonpublic schools are operated by Catholic, Missouri Synod Lutheran, Orthodox Jewish, Christian Reformed, and various fundamentalist denominations and congregations. These schools, reflecting the views of their owners, generally teach that abortion is a grave sin and that women should not be ordained to the clergy. Many of these schools also teach that contraception is immoral and that women should generally be subordinate to men.

So long as these schools are funded by private donations or tuition charges, they may teach as they please. But when they receive any public funding whatever, women—and men who support women's rights—are taxed to subsidize instruction that undermines the rights of women.

DOUBLE TAXATION

A favorite argument of parochiaid promoters has it that patrons of nonpublic schools are double-taxed, once for the public schools and again for their own private schools. But that simply will not wash. Whatever anyone pays to a private school is a voluntary donation or voluntary tuition payment.

Double taxation is, however, a good argument against parochiaid, although perhaps it should be termed multi-taxation. Voucher or tuition tax credit support of nonpublic schools would mean that citizens are taxed not only to support the public schools which they control through elected school boards but also the Catholic, Missouri Synod Lutheran, Christian Reformed, Orthodox Jewish, Muslim, fundamentalist, and other private schools.

A central idea behind tax-supported public education is that the public interest in an educated citizenry and an educated work force is so compelling that all taxpayers must contribute their share, whether they have children or not, to religiously neutral institutions open to all and governed by elected representatives of the people.

FREE EXERCISE OF RELIGION

Some parochiaid advocates claim that their constitutional right to the free exercise of religion is impaired or violated if they have to shoulder the whole financial burden of denominational day schools. We cannot agree. We believe that this argument is analogous to saying that freedom of the press requires that government provide us with tax-paid print or electronic media for expression, or that free exercise of religion requires government to build churches for us.

Free exercise of religion means that government may not interfere with the exercise of our religion, unless that free exercise threatens the equal rights of others (a religious belief in slavery or human sacrifice may not be acted upon) or government has a legitimate and compelling reason to interfere, as, for instance, to prohibit preaching with a bullhorn at 3:00 A.M. in a residential neighborhood.

The obligation of government to free exercise is fulfilled simply by allowing religious schools to operate. Tax support for them would violate every person's right not to be taxed for the support of any religion, including one's own. As Benjamin Franklin wisely pointed out: "When a religion is good, I conceive it will support itself; and when it does not support itself, and God does not take care to support it so that its professors are obliged to call for help of the civil power, 'tis a sign, I apprehend, of its being a bad one."

IS AMERICA OUT OF STEP?

Parochiaid propagandists often call attention to the fact that other industrial countries provide tax support for nonpublic schools, implying that the United States is out of step with those countries and should emulate them. It is true that some countries do tax their citizens to support sectarian and other private schools, but our country would be foolish to imitate them blindly.

All the countries providing tax support for nonpublic schools either have a history of established churches or were set up by countries with such histories. Countries with parochiaid tend to be much less religiously pluralistic than the United States, often as a result of their historical church-state union policies. So for the considerably more pluralistic United States to adopt parochiaid would be to invite a much greater degree of social fragmentation than is the case in the less pluralistic countries. When the Netherlands, for instance, began parochiaid during World War I, its educational system split into three basic columns—public, Catholic, and Calvinist. A similar policy in the United States would lead to horrendous fragmentation in education.

Political struggles over parochiaid have been very divisive. France and Belgium have had riots, demonstrations, and strikes over parochiaid. The attempt by the Spanish Republic (1931–1936) to separate church and state and advance religious liberty was one of the causes of General Franco's military revolt against the elected government (1936–1939). Australia was torn by political strife over parochiaid for years during the 1960s and 1970s. Tax-supported religious segregation in Northern Ireland is one important factor in the sectarian violence there.

In neighboring Canada tax support of sectarian schools has prevented the development of public education in the provinces of Quebec and Newfoundland. In Ontario, Catholic schools receive tax support while Protestant and Jewish schools do not, which is a constant source of friction. In Great Britain traditional tax support for Protestant and Catholic schools has encouraged Muslims, Hindus, Rastafarians, and others to seek the same privileges.

Given this we may be permitted to generalize, therefore, that in every country in which it is government policy to provide tax support for private schools, religious divisions and divisiveness are encouraged, educational efficiency is reduced, and citizens are not protected against taxes for religion.

We Americans should be proud that our country pioneered the church-state separation principle that has given us more religious freedom than any other country and has made it possible for so many diverse religious groups to live together in reasonable harmony.

INTERFERENCE IN CHURCH AFFAIRS

Tax support of sectarian private schools will inevitably mean government involvement and entanglement in the internal affairs of the religious bodies that operate private schools. There is considerable debate within the churches which operate schools over the desirability of separate full-time day schools as vehicles of religious education. Government support, therefore, skews the debate in favor of those intrachurch factions which favor having private schools. This is particularly true for Roman Catholics.

During the 1960s and thereafter, many sincere Catholics advocated the reduction or elimination of parochial schools. They argued for greater church attention to the great majority of Catholic students who attend public schools and whose religious education was limited to Confraternity of Christian Doctrine (CCD) classes in local parishes. Many Catholic reformers also sought a reallocation of financial priorities in the parishes, with more expenditures for charitable activities. Other Catholics argued that parochial schools belonged to another era in American life, when a defensive posture was felt to be necessary to counteract the larger society's not infrequent anti-Catholicism. All those groups had their articulate spokespersons.

In her book *Are Parochial Schools the Answer?* author, mother, and Catholic convert Mary Perkins Ryan argued that parochial education was anachronistic. It detracted from the parish liturgy and adult education by making the school the center of parish life.[19] She also argued that Catholics had assimilated well into American society and no longer needed a separate vehicle to protect an immigrant community from a hostile environment. Her views were reinforced somewhat by studies concluding that Catholic schools were no longer necessary for the church's survival."[20]

Both Cardinal Joseph Ritter of St. Louis and Bishop Ernest J. Primeau of the National Catholic Educational Association openly suggested that parochial schools may not be desirable for the long-term goals of the church.[21] James C. Donohue estimated in 1968 that parochial schools accounted for half the annual expenditures of the nation's nearly 18,000 parishes. He argued for a change in church priorities.[22]

The intrachurch debate appears to have been won by those supporting the maintenance of a separate school system, though Catholic school enrollment has declined by half since 1965 and Catholic dissatisfaction with church management has reached high levels. But the involvement of government, through legislative actions and funding schemes, may have been a crucial factor in sustaining the institutionalists. It was clearly improper for government to involve itself in the internal affairs of ecclesiastical groups. It is not the government's business to save parochial schools, as President Richard Nixon pledged to the Knights of Columbus in 1972; nor should the government try to drive them out of business.

PRIVATE SCHOOL AUTONOMY

Nonpublic schools' much-prized independence and autonomy would be threatened by acceptance of large-scale public funding. That danger is a clear and direct one. What government supports, government controls. This is an ancient axiom repeatedly ratified by experience. Nothing in recent U.S. political history suggests otherwise.

It is inevitable, too, that the taxpaying public will want some say in the hiring of faculty, the educational standards of the church school, the educational qualifications of faculty and administrators, and other matters as well. This influence will inevitably increase as public funds flow into these institutions.

Monsignor Thomas J. Curry saw this threat clearly in a recent article: "There is simply no possibility that Catholic education can receive substantial public assistance and that the church can at the same time maintain complete control and direction of its schools. The reception of public monies must inevitably involve public supervision or control. . . . The greatest danger for Catholic schools is that they may fail to secure public assistance, but that in order to receive such aid they may secularize themselves piecemeal in the process. . . ."[23]

Observed Justice William J. Brennan: "When a sectarian institution accepts state financial aid, it becomes obligated under the Equal Protection clause of the Fourteenth Amendment not to discriminate in admissions policies and faculty selection."[24] Even Chief Justice William Rehnquist, the leading parochiaider on the Court, said bluntly in a 1986 case, "Even religious schools cannot claim to be wholly free from state regulation."[25]

Indeed, as is well known, acceptance of tax aid has led to the secularization of many church-related colleges and universities. Speaking at a conference at Fordham University in April 1991, Jesuit theologian Avery Dulles talked about the "slippery path" that led universities such as Harvard, Yale, Princeton, and Chicago "from denominational to generic Christianity, then to vaguely defined religious values, and finally to total secularization." Dulles added that "many competent observers are of the opinion that this drift is by now inevitable in practically all Catholic universities."[26]

PLURALISM AND DIVERSITY

Parochiaid advocates often insist that voucher or tuition tax credit support of nonpublic schools is necessary if we are to preserve pluralism and diversity in our society. They frequently couple this argument with criticism of what they call the "government monopoly" in education.

But where is the individual student more likely to be exposed to pluralism and diversity? In nonpublic schools, with their tendency toward religious homogeneity and narrower, generally sectarian curricula, with their academic selectivity on the secondary level, and disinclination to serve handicapped children? Or will the student encounter more pluralism and diversity in our public schools, with their rich mix of students and staff of every religion, race, social class, and national background? The answer is obvious.

As for the monopoly accusation, it hardly seems to fit a system in which nearly 16,000 local public school districts are governed by elected boards of local parents and taxpayers, subject to broad state guidelines and constitutional restrictions designed to protect the rights of individual students.

THE G.I. BILL ANALOGY

Advocates of parochiaid often analogize tax aid for sectarian elementary and secondary schools to the G.I. Bills which funded post-secondary education for veterans of World War II and the Korean War in both public and nonpublic institutions. The analogy breaks down, however, when it is recognized that the G.I. Bills were not intended as support for institutions, but, rather, as compensation to men and women who had served in the armed forces and whose civilian educations and careers had been interrupted by their military service.

"SECULAR HUMANISM"

Some parochiaiders charge that public schools teach the "religion of secular humanism" and, therefore, it would be only fair for government to support nonpublic schools which teach some variety of Christianity.

If, indeed, some public schools teach the "religion of secular humanism," then the sensible thing to do is not to compound the problem by providing tax support for schools teaching other religions, but to terminate the teaching of the "religion of secular humanism."

The trouble with all this is that those who make the charge define "secular humanism" so loosely and so broadly that the term has little meaning. "Secular humanism" to these critics is often just a catch-all term for everything they do not like in public schools, from sex education to Hemingway novels to evolution to home economics to the relative scarcity of material about religion in social studies textbooks. It is charged, for instance, that science classes teach evolution and humanists believe in evolution; therefore, the schools are teaching humanism. Humanists also believe in democracy, but that does not mean that civics, history, and government classes that teach democracy are teaching humanism. It just happens that most educated Catholics, Protestants, and Jews have no quarrel with evolution and do not object to its being taught in science classes.

There is, of course, a religion or philosophy or life stance called humanism (or Humanism). Several million Americans are probably humanists, though specifically humanist organizations (such as the American Humanist Association, the Council for Democratic and Secular Humanism, the American Ethical Union, the Society for Humanistic Judaism, and many Unitarian Universalist congregations) have fewer than a quarter million aggregate members. In any event, what distinguishes humanists from moderate to liberal Christians and Jews is a naturalistic ethical philosophy that does not include a belief in a deity or personal survival after death. We know of no American public school that has espoused that position.

It is proper, of course, for the courts to consider the charge that public schools teach the "religion of secular humanism." That indeed occurred in the 1980s in Alabama in *Smith* v. *Board of School Commissioners of Mobile County*. Fundamentalist plaintiffs charged the local public schools with "the unconstitutional advancement of the religion of Humanism" and the "unconstitutional violation of the free exercise of religious rights of teachers and students by the exclusive teaching of Humanism and the systematic exclusion from the curriculum of the existence, history, and contributions and role of Christianity in the United States and the world." Federal District Judge W. Brevard Hand ruled in 1987 in favor of the plaintiffs and ordered 44 history, social studies, and home economics texts removed from all Alabama schools for allegedly teaching "secular humanism."

Judge Hand held that the scarcity of references to religion in the texts amounted to teaching "secular humanism," though he gave no hint as to how many or what kind of references to religion would be considered adequate. He also held that the home economics texts promoted "secular humanism" by encouraging adolescents to learn to think and to make decisions in real-life situations.

Judge Hand's ruling was overturned by the Eleventh Circuit U.S. Court of Appeals five months later. The appellate court saw no need to offer a definition of religion, but held, "We find that, even assuming that secular humanism is a religion for purposes of the establishment clause, Appellees [the fundamentalist plaintiffs] have failed to prove a violation of the establishment clause" through use of the challenged textbooks. The court added that "use of the challenged textbooks has the primary effect of conveying information that is essentially neutral in its religious content to the school children who utilize the books; none of these books convey a message of governmental approval of secular humanism or government disapproval of theism."[27]

Further, the appellate court held, the home economics books do not endorse "secular humanism or any other religion. Rather, the message conveyed is one of a governmental attempt to instill in Alabama public school children such values as independent thought, tolerance of diverse views, self-respect, maturity, self-reliance and logical decision making. This is an entirely appropriate secular effect. . . . Nor do these textbooks evidence an attitude antagonistic to theistic belief."[28]

Of the history books, the court said, "There is simply nothing in this record to indicate that omission of certain facts regarding religion from these textbooks of itself constituted an advancement of secular humanism or an active hostility toward theistic religion prohibited by the establishment clause."[29]

The U.S. Supreme Court declined to review the appellate ruling.

Those who charge that humanism is either taught in or is the "established religion" of the public schools have failed to prove that charge because the charge is without substance; therefore, it can hardly stand up as an argument for tax aid for church schools.

IS OPPOSING PAROCHIAID ANTI-CATHOLIC?

Although the accusation is heard less frequently now than when Catholic schools made up the vast majority of nonpublic schools, parochiaiders have insisted that opposition to tax support for nonpublic schools is motivated by anti-Catholic bias. That this charge is rarely true is shown by the fact that many prominent Catholics have opposed parochiaid, among them the late President John F. Kennedy, Senator Edward Kennedy, former Supreme Court Justice William J. Brennan, and former National Education Association President John Ryor. In every referendum on parochiaid the returns show that substantial numbers of Catholics voted against aid. This was especially notable in the Massachusetts referenda in the 1980s.

Further, opposition to parochiaid is not confined to tax support of Catholic schools. Rather, it is a principled opposition to tax aid for any nonpublic schools—Catholic, Protestant, Jewish, Muslim, or whatever—and a principled support for public schools, which enroll three-quarters of Catholic children, and the constitutional principle of separation of church and state.

SEMANTIC SWITCH

In order to make parochiaid more palatable, some of its promoters have proposed labeling as public schools all schools that are "open to the public." Thus, a sectarian school advertising itself as being "open to the public" could claim tax support.

This ploy is too transparent to take in anyone but the most gullible. What makes a school public is not only public funding and a willingness to consider all applicants. To be genuinely public, a school must be completely under public control, free of any kind of religious, ethnic, gender, or ideological discrimination in admissions and hiring, and free of any sort of religious indoctrination. Obviously, no nonpublic school that values religious and other distinctions is likely to abandon them for Caesar's coin.

ECUMENISM

We sometimes hear it said that opposition to parochiaid is "unecumenical" or that it promotes discord among people of differing faiths. Upon examination this accusation is clearly absurd.

What is truly unecumenical is to divide children by creed in church schools and then have government force all citizens to support those institutions.

The political campaigns to secure passage of legislation in order to provide involuntary tax support for sectarian schools have proven to be divisive, tearing the fabric of society along denominational lines, and disrupting good relations within faith groups.

EDUCATIONAL IMPROVEMENT

Advocates of tax support for nonpublic schools (most of them lawyers, economists, columnists, clergy, and special interest lobbyists, but rarely teachers) are fond of claiming that tax-supported choice among public and nonpublic schools will result in better education. They go on a great deal about moving students and teachers around, which will increase the costs of education, but they seldom make specific suggestions as to how education can be improved for Johnny or Janie.

Parochiaiders often point to the fact that many, if not most, nonpublic schools spend less money per student than public schools and send a higher percentage of them on to college. But as we have shown elsewhere, nonpublic schools tend to cost less because they pay teachers less, offer fewer educational services, and serve far fewer handicapped or otherwise disadvantaged children, for whom instructional services cost considerably more. They send a higher percentage of graduates to college largely because they are academically selective to begin with, and because they cater to families with average incomes higher than that of the average public school family (educational achievement being roughly proportional to family income).

While tax-supported public and nonpublic school choice will shuffle students and teachers round, perhaps with often dismaying and disruptive rapidity, and raise school costs, it cannot itself guarantee any improvement in education.

Educators know how education can and should be improved. Head Start and Chapter I remedial education programs need to be fully funded. Class sizes need to be reduced, especially for disadvantaged children. School-based day care would reduce some of the problems of latchkey children. Further, education would be improved if the social pathologies associated with poverty and inner-city infrastructural deterioration were to be treated. The unfortunate situation now is that many inner-city children come malnourished to broken-down, dirty, vermin-infested schools where they have to use worn-out and outdated textbooks, while drug dealers and criminals prowl the nearby streets.

Above all, what American education needs is national and local political and public commitment to giving public education high priority. If our society can enjoy luxuries unheard of but a few generations ago, surely it can find the resources to provide such necessities as good education for all American children. This can and should be done without the costly, divisive, unconstitutional, and unnecessary diversion of public funds to nonpublic schools.

NOTES

1. John E. Chubb and Terry M. Doe, *Politics, Markets, and America's Schools* (Washington, D.C.: Brookings Institute, 1990).

2. Justice Hugo L. Black for the majority, 330 U.S. 15, 16.

3. Ibid. at 18.

4. Ibid. at 31, 32.

5. Ibid. at 59.

6. Ibid. at 60.

7. 105 S. Ct. 2479 (1985).

8. C. Herman Pritchett, *The American Constitution*, 3rd ed. (New York: McGraw Hill, 1977), p. 401.

9. John M. Swomley, *Religious Liberty and the Secular State* (Buffalo, N.Y.: Prometheus Books, 1987), pp. 43–49.

10. Ibid., p. 49.

11. Florence Flast, "Why Parochiaid is a Threat to Public Education and Religious Liberty," statement issued June 12, 1972.

12. *The Living Church*, Editorial, April 21, 1974.

13. James S. Catterall, *Tuition Tax Credits: Fact and Fiction* (Bloomington, Ind.: Phi Delta Kappa Educational Foundation, 1983), p. 33.

14. Ibid., p. 34.

15. Ibid., p. 26.

16. 330 US 53, 54.

17. *Board of Education* v. *Allen*, 391 U.S. 254.

18. "Postscript on the Blaine Amendment," *Christianity and Crisis* 27 (October 30, 1967): 242.

19. Mary Perkins Ryan, *Are Parochial Schools the Answer?* (New York: Holt, Rinehart & Winston, 1964).

20. Andrew M. Greeley and Peter H. Rossi, *The Education of Catholic Americans* (Hawthorne, N.Y.: Aldine, 1966), and Reginald A. Neuwein, ed., *Catholic Schools in Action* (Notre Dame, Ind.: University of Notre Dame, 1966).

21. *National Catholic Press Reporter*, September 27, 1967.

22. "New Priorities in Catholic Education," *America* 118 (April 13, 1968): 476–79.

23. "Aid to Catholic Education," *America* 154 (April 5, 1986): 277–78.

24. *Lemon* v. *Kurtzman*, 403 U.S. 622.

25. *Ohio Civil Rights Commission* v. *Dayton Christian Schools*, (1986), 476 US 1103.

26. *New York Times*, May 1, 1991, p. A1.

27. 827 F.2d. 684.

28. Ibid.

29. Ibid.

Appendix:

Supplementary Tables

TABLE 10

ABOVE AVERAGE CATHOLIC SCHOOL
ENROLLMENT STATES, 1969–70

1.	Pennsylvania	17.2%
2.	Rhode Island	16.8%
3.	New Jersey	16.5%
4.	New York	16.3%
5.	Illinois	15.2%
6.	Massachusetts	14.2%
7.	Wisconsin	14.2%
8.	New Hampshire	13.8%
9.	Connecticut	12.2%
10.	Louisiana	12.2%
11.	Ohio	12.0%
12.	Delaware	11.6%
13.	Nebraska	11.6%
National Average		9.1%

Source: *Quality Education Data* (Denver 1990)

TABLE 11

ABOVE AVERAGE CATHOLIC SCHOOL
ENROLLMENT STATES, 1989–90

1.	Pennsylvania	12.8%
2.	Rhode Island	12.2%
3.	Illinois	12.1%
4.	New Jersey	11.7%
5.	New York	10.7%
6.	Delaware	10.7%
7.	Louisiana	10.3%
8.	Wisconsin	9.4%
9.	Ohio	9.3%
10.	Massachusetts	9.3%
11.	Connecticut	9.2%
12.	Missouri	9.1%
13.	Nebraska	9.0%
National Average		9.1%

Source: *Quality Education Data* (Denver 1990)

TABLE 12

TOTAL ELEMENTARY AND SECONDARY ENROLLMENTS, 1989–90

	Enrollments				Percentages		
State	Public	Catholic	Other Nonpublic	Total	Public	Catholic	Other Non-public
Alab.	728,394	13,403	48,897	790,694	92.1%	1.7%	6.2%
Alas.	103,402	917	4,065	108,348	95.4%	0.8%	3.8%
Ariz.	598,056	16,654	30,674	645,382	92.6%	2.6%	4.8%
Ark.	439,205	7,033	11,199	457,437	96.1%	1.5%	2.4%
Calif.	4,606,804	245,546	287,098	5,139,448	89.6%	4.8%	5.6%
Colo.	564,634	16,363	21,056	602,056	93.8%	2.7%	3.5%
Conn.	461,773	49,783	28,334	539,890	85.6%	9.2%	5.2%
Del.	95,969	12,630	9,822	118,421	81.0%	10.7%	8.3%
D.C.	89,043	9,283	8,400	106,726	83.4%	8.7%	7.9%
Fla.	1,683,357	69,542	159,845	1,912,744	88.0%	3.6%	8.4%
Geog.	1,106,316	11,559	78,626	1,196,501	92.4%	1.0%	6.6%
Haw.	168,298	13,002	22,394	203,694	82.6%	6.4%	11.0%
Id.	208,994	2,217	4,445	215,666	96.9%	1.0%	2.1%
Ill.	1,826,016	261,787	77,309	2,165,112	84.3%	12.1%	3.6%
Ind.	969,225	55,556	46,911	1,071,692	90.4%	5.2%	4.4%
Iowa	482,680	39,300	11,594	533,574	90.4%	7.4%	2.2%
Kans.	420,696	25,524	10,382	456,602	92.1%	5.6%	2.3%
Ken.	671,357	44,677	16,962	732,996	91.6%	6.1%	2.3%
La.	811,641	98,419	46,053	956,113	84.9%	10.3%	4.8%
Me.	210,315	5,295	10,953	226,563	92.9%	2.3%	4.8%
Md.	691,568	57,864	58,042	807,474	85.6%	7.2%	7.2%
Mass.	846,576	92,445	52,448	991,469	85.4%	.3%	5.3%
Mich.	1,623,938	110,235	85,956	1,820,119	89.2%	6.1%	4.7%
Minn.	734,046	55,275	30,442	819,760	89.6%	6.7%	3.7%
Miss.	490,809	10,274	37,132	538,215	91.2%	1.9%	6.9%

TABLE 12 (CONT.)

	Enrollments				Percentages		
State	Public	Catholic	Other Nonpublic	Total	Public	Catholic	Other Non-public
Mo.	816,037	84,842	33,648	934,527	87.3%	9.1%	3.6%
Mont.	156,899	3,557	3,964	164,420	95.4%	2.2%	2.4%
Neb.	268,213	27,258	8,360	303,831	88.2%	9.0%	2.8%
Nev.	166,634	4,615	4,440	175,689	94.9%	2.6%	2.5%
N.H.	163,571	8,938	11,550	184,005	88.8%	4.9%	6.3%
N.J.	1,136,850	157,430	46,736	1,341,016	84.8%	11.7%	3.5%
N.M.	277,344	9,058	10,050	296,452	93.5%	3.1%	3.4%
N.Y.	2,627,690	335,627	186,059	3,149,376	83.4%	10.7%	5.9%
N.C.	1,102,072	8,727	48,585	1,159,384	95.0%	0.8%	4.2%
N.D.	117,847	6,509	1,606	125,962	93.5%	5.2%	1.3%
Oh.	1,829,037	192,913	49,089	2,071,039	88.3%	9.3%	2.4%
Okla.	614,327	7,764	12,007	634,098	96.9%	1.2%	1.9%
Ore.	456,905	11,185	19,653	487,743	93.7%	2.3%	4.0%
Penn.	1,708,249	265,890	99,178	2,073,317	82.4%	12.8%	4.8%
R.I.	135,697	19,504	4,730	159,931	84.8%	12.2%	3.0%
S.C.	620,877	6,254	45,563	672,694	92.3%	0.9%	6.8%
S.D.	127,469	6,121	3,213	136,803	93.2%	4.5%	2.3%
Tenn.	827,297	13,340	47,600	888,237	93.1%	1.5%	5.4%
Tex.	3,223,610	70,491	127,599	3,421,699	94.2%	2.1%	3.7%
Utah	419,494	3,638	3,358	426,490	98.3%	0.9%	0.8%
Vt.	92,974	3,151	3,922	100,047	93.0%	3.1%	3.9%
Virg.	999,758	21,073	64,411	1,085,242	92.2%	1.9%	5.9%
Wash.	759,734	22,245	38,825	820,804	92.6%	2.7%	4.7%
W.V.	358,194	6,934	5,990	371,118	96.5%	1.9%	1.6%
Wisc.	802,144	88,906	54,756	945,806	84.8%	9.4%	5.8%
Wyom.	95,320	1,229	1,283	97,832	97.4%	1.3%	1.3%

Source: *Quality Education Data* (Denver 1990)

Index